CW00688777

The Water Engine

Ankh Spice

Collected Poems

Advance Praise for *The Water Engine:*

"Ankh Spice's *The Water Engine* is a stunning collection of poems that perhaps does not appreciate its own power. It is brimming with naturalistic beauty, with humility, with raw emotion, and with exquisite skill. The ebb and flow of the texts perfectly represent the subject matter and Spice's employment of imagery is simultaneously creative and evocative. Other poets have written about the oceans, but few with such a keen eye. Indeed, Spice's voice is entirely unique, to the point that it could be said that even the ancient form of the haiku is reinvented here. This collection juxtaposes the austere, with rich detail, and manages to maintain a common theme throughout. Moreover, there is a candour about this work, a purity. This is expertly written, beautifully framed, must-read poetry from a poet operating at their peak."

—Alan Parry, Co-Founding Editor of The Broken Spine
& author of *Neon Ghosts*

"There are tricks so profound, we reel at their grace– Ankh Spice writes in his extraordinary and richly lyrical new book *The Water Engine.* He is referring to the tides, the skill of the sea, but this gifted and empathic poet could be talking about his own work (if he weren't so humble) and alluding to a mastery of image, sound, and an uncanny ability to capture the world's wonders, delights and sorrows on the page. These are spellbinding and immersive poems, brave and bold and big enough to celebrate love, mourn losses, and pay homage to nature in all its manifestations. To read *The Water Engine* is to look at the winter sun on the incoming tide, and to be dazzled. When the poet writes 'I too was once a strong magic spell just barely contained inside a skin' we believe him."

—Anna Saunders, author of *Feverfew*
& founder of the Cheltenham Poetry Festival

"Denise Levertov, quoting Schweitzer, tells us that "Attention is the exercise of Reverence for the 'other forms of life that want to live.'" In *The Water Engine*, Ankh Spice pays careful and sustained attention in the service of reverence for life in all its forms. This intense focus of all his senses on our world (and in some cases what's missing from it), combined with his polished unfolding of words and their music, compels and sharpens the reader's own reverence toward everything in it."

—Lee Potts, poetry editor, *Barren Magazine*
& author of *And Drought Will Follow*

"Every page of Ankh Spice's *The Water Engine* makes me feel like I am barely treading water. This collection is dense and relentless, and I'm a little afraid of the hungry tentacle lurking beneath the murky surface. 'I have swum out deep,' Spice writes, and I prepare for the undertow, heavy with stubborn survival. When poetry is great, it can sometimes be mistaken for drowning."

—Lannie Stabile, author of *Good Morning to Everyone Except Men Who Name Their Dogs Zeus*

"It's so rare that I encounter a book of poetry that reshapes how I think of language, and of form, and of the wonder that is our human spirit. Ankh Spice's new collection, *The Water Engine*, is exactly that book. Every page feels elemental to life, bringing water, fire, wind, and heavy earth to us line by line. These poems swim in rough waters and in calm. They dance to minor keys and in rays of light. Language, movement, mythology, ocean, wind, salvation—Ankh Spice delivers it all to us here in such pristine voice we can't help but be transformed."

—Jack B. Bedell, author of *Color All Maps New,*
Poet Laureate, State of Louisiana, 2017-2019

"There is something prophetic in the controlled chaos of Ankh's writing. It is an intangible, unnameable, and ancient impulse that carries these poems along. The organization of this collection is a sort of debrief as each reader becomes a part of the experiment of how water works. The Intake prepares us for transformation, 'out here surely I'm the thing caught / between states. Not swimmer not floater. / Pushed upward by water, weighed down / by air, no longer fish but still wearing / the shapes of fins[.]' The Engine tells us what to expect of the device, in every sense of the word, 'we'll be travelling light, so there'll be time for that road.' The Blockage is how it can all go wrong, 'the weight of the world cracks your careful shell.' The Whoosh is a flight, 'feel your shape made to float free / you perfect engine / from all the mud / that ever denied you air.' And The Drift is the unresolving end to a water cycle, 'this light, it may change any moment.' The cycles in this collection are as reliable as waves— churning in relation to a controlling moon. Her pull divines each sentiment, and sometimes there are riptides, or collapsed oceanic shelves, sometimes a volcano, or an earthquake, but it all steadies back to the invoked, and intricate process. Each piece carries its crucial place. Like the universe—it's organized chaos. But somehow, the chaos loves and is loved. The grateful link to the immensity of the erratic sea is truly the gift of this collection. We are better for this generosity."

—Kari Flickinger, author of *The Gull and the Bell Tower*

"There are people who write poetry and then there are poets. Simply poets. Those people placed among us to record the flight, fight and plight. This is one of those poets. Ankh Spice dives further into the darkness so that we don't have to and this Atlantis of a collection is what he has brought back up. A masterpiece of storytelling, time travel and the disassembling of the human spirit. Written with honesty, humility and the brutality endured in living on the edge of the void, this is a densely atmospheric collection exploring our relationship to sea, shore and self. This is no 'quiet, ordinary tide', but a 'sea monster', revealing, amid deeply personal poems, the 'wounded ape' in all of us, 'calling, calling'. A unique collection from an exceptional writer, best appreciated between 'breast and crawl.'"

—Damien B. Donnelly,
host & producer, *Eat The Storms Poetry Podcast*
& author of *Enough*

"When so much contemporary poetry occupies itself with peripherals, here is a book which flies 'carrier-witted' to the very centre of it all, and addresses fears and desires and hypocrisies head-on. Unselfconscious & with little concern for hollow poetic effects or the glorification of ego, Spice exhibits a Keatsian negative capability which is always attuned to the natural world in which we humans live and move and have our being, and always attuned and compassionate to other humans sharing the space. Coming out of Aotearoa, this extraordinarily powerful— prophetic— book will have an influence which extends far beyond those potent ancient spirit-islands, and will carry 'healing in its wings'.

This is serious poetry. The sea—no cliché or bit part here but a main agent—surrounds, envelops, floods the body and psyche. Bodies are focal—they are cities, landscapes, addresses ('Turns out we're all a less desirable address/ than the one advertised./But let's move in./Let's move/in these bodies scraped back from the edge,/let's move with intent/to take up space.')

The refusal which is expressed in the opening poem— 'I do not wish to should, I will not give/the cunning of my cogs to this unmagic' ('For what, this water engine?')—runs like a spine through this substantial and powerful book. There are totally immersive and exhilarating linguistic effects of language– gambolling play and collision in the manner of Gerard Manley Hopkins and Dylan Thomas, wresting new meanings from old words, and yet explosively, compassionately, reinventively, of today. One poem is self-awarely described by the poet as being 'inspired by the sensation' which 'Dylan Thomas metres out inside an atypical brain'.

Most of all this is a celebration: of place, of ancestors, of true roots, the natural elements; of human vulnerability and resilience; language, myth, magic, gratitude— to quote the aforementioned Hopkins, of 'dappled things... All things counter, original, spare, strange;/Whatever is fickle, freckled (who knows how?)/...swift, slow; sweet, sour; adazzle....',: *life* in all its bustling teeming unexpected joyous exuberance."

—Geraldine Clarkson, author of *Monica's Overcoat of Flesh* and *Crucifox*

"In this comprehensive and mighty debut collection, *The Water Engine*, Ankh Spice stands shoulder to shoulder with poets, such as Les Murray, e.e. cummings, Hart Crane and Dylan Thomas in breaking and remaking language to transport the reader to visionary landscapes, mind-altering terrain and as-yet unarticulated, unchartered emotional territories. Many of the poems are elegies for the 'wounded ape' in us all and there are truly haunting, if not harrowing, moments in this work, the 'long voyages back to darkness' where mental health and life's adversities are examined forensically, a disorder of the senses that is as disturbing as it is mesmerising. Though we are 'ghosts in waiting', heard as 'a constant howl' from space, Spice dazzles us with the 'quartz pricked glitter' of his vivid and imagery. *The Water Engine* deserves to be a seminal poetic text of our generation."

—Matthew M. C. Smith, editor, *Black Bough Poetry* & author of *Origin: 21 Poems*

The
Water Engine

Ankh Spice

Collected Poems

Spice /Ankh, author

The Water Engine / Ankh Spice

Poems

ISBN: 978-1-7365167-5-1

Library of Congress Control Number: 2021949531

Edited by: Elisabeth Horan & Amanda McLeod
Book Design: Amanda McLeod
Cover Art: Anna Spence
Art Photography: Keli Watson
Cover Design: Amanda McLeod

PUBLISHER

Femme Salvé Books
An Imprint of Animal Heart Press

P.O. Box 322
Thetford Center, Vermont 05075
https://femmesalvébooks.net

For Caitlin,
who billows with me in the wind
for as long as we circle

For Diana,
whose songs and stories were the first water

And for you,
all you ambulant seas, taking it all in,
flinging your shoulds to the whoosh.
May you return to the source
drifting
and light
and unafraid

Table Of Contents

The Intake

For what, this water engine?

Run this day untracked, this stolen day —
derailed, spilled
oil for us who tender
our machinery at a limp
until the chug of it smuts us
—should-should-should—

How do we should, when the light lances
tremolo beams, crooning out
from the riddled body of the earth

How can I should, when this gutter puddle
stuns herself giddy gold
with the systole pump of the sun

I do not wish to should, I will not give
the cunning of my cogs to this unmagic
but run until unwound, supping
drowse and honey-dapple

And if I must become some grinding thing again
take my rivet-flanks for a fountain — pointless
but for urging the water
to dance with the water

A place to stand, a lever

On the beach, three children have conjured
a world. The castle survived an afternoon

century of siege, and is ancient now, shadow
longing toward the water. A fence of feathers

is still flying a boundary between his necessary
graveyard, her garden. Careful seashell tombstones

and careful seashell pathways, from this angle
shine the same – white bone, broken patterns.

The youngest child, banished for the chaos he carried
so loosely, terraformed the badlands at the edge

of the tide. That far country is dangerous, tunnel
and collapse, channel and mountain. But the three

are safe in the tearooms, powers combined to manifest
ice-cream. It does not matter to them now

that the great flood they surely knew was coming,
is coming. The driftwood has sailed too long

and is heavy, and who can ever carry enough
for a buttress, and who could ever dam away

a whole sea, but one long piece it leaps to the hand
like a wand. And I do believe that I too,

I too was once a strong magic spell
just barely contained inside a skin.

The body is a wave

This morning you made for the bright water
    like it was your mother, she who first knew your body

        as a wave, read your floated comma
           of spine and shadow. How right that we still use our salts

            to remember, a wet grey sponge
                to forget. We dive for the once-boat and once

           I too was unfinished ribs. The jealous sea
    had already wrecked the knot in my chest

her own creature
    for the long voyage back to darkness, said ah but here

        is a wave who will break, and break, like he might dance
          correctly, meaning arms, hands

           become small flights of gulls – swoop
              and fall, traceries – a dropped heartbeat on a screen

           maps across long pale paper
    as tidelines on the sand, as conducted birds.

Would that my bones, my beat
    had stayed buoyant enough to rhythm

        the foam-line, the screeling sky, but as we surface
          right this second on your nape the light describes

a flare, a droplet, a lighthouse warning
tender rock of vertebra, star-pulse, strobe-syncope

and I cling to you and we are a wave
and a particle – simultaneous and all-at-once and what we are now

will last less than a breath

will explain the machine of the sun

Ninth wave (IV: finale, D minor)

At centre, the wishing-
pin, the sternum. Dear rudder, tidy prow
that sails us true – you know that when the big waves hit, we break
them with the heart. And how flexible, the shield
so strong it gives enough
to quiver, bouncing strike after strike of the bell inside
the cage. Oh note, oh note, oh love, oh listen,
you've been filling up with music since the start. Your palm
is shaped to press the keel, to find the hidden
catch, and if you steer a vessel tenderly
that way, it creaks wide open
like a door – we're all born knocking
from inside. Then what floods from the chest is yours and yours
alone – plainsong of sun
through synapse, a galloping light
that flares each crest to foaming flame. Drum-scud
of the bow, the whoop,
the skirl, the flood that brims the sea inside
to overflow. And long ago a sailing man
who couldn't hear, he found that hinge, cracked free
the rolling light-
made-sound that filled him beautiful
and netted it in his ode. Our mouths, they still
go round to show we feel
all of the impossible.
Don't try, don't try now
to explain, I know: the time, the flow, the phrase. The key
slid major, the state of this hollow instrument. Nothing matters now
but the breve – our shivering
moment of sustain.

Making waves

The bay curves her back, soft hands
of spume all stroke
for the ache. What clicks *just so*
is tender, as carefully stretched to relief
as all you've carried for eighty years
for this coast, and the sea nestles into you
both just the same – still the fretty child.
And there's no possible unravelling, no cord
to cut – yes you can say *ocean*
and you can say *dune* but they're each the stuff
of the other, the salt that stars herself
through the sand, that sand whose cells
are quartz-pricked glitter, churned in turn to silver up
the pulse-line of crests, then the valve dips
the interval and whatever falls shining
in the dark becomes foundation – critical
slopes for the whittle of sun-greedy waves. Easy to forget
what lays itself down makes the roll. And you are in the grit
and the shape of this shell that carries me on
and you are the rill in the vein, every plucked string always
playing you out here, from the click of bruit and beyond
your fret. Echo back to the sounds that timbred the shape
of your spine to answer her best to that old hard wind
and in this way we know who we are. That we fall
with foundation. That every grain of us
settles right here always
tilting the chin of each new wave, up, up,
up. That the light's lip quivers, then defines.

Four haiku (one lie, three moons)

Each night the sea lies

to the shore –*I would not change*

you for all the world

Impatient the moon

tears down her mourning curtains

and paints on surprise

She arrives early

wearing daybirds for lashes

shy of the bright sea

Milkmother moon drips

sustenance, every hill

drinks giddy her sup

After the solstice swim

At the scribbled tideline   we gather   with wax hands

long bones of the floaters   brittle femurs   the white moon's jawbone

a snapped rib   what isn't boomed hollow now   hungry

for the burning   flotsam, scoured thin   months treading the swells

worn fibres, tired touchpaper   best for beachfire   you cracked lip

of land   craving smoke tongues   to lick salt-glitter grudging

from seven newborn sister stars

rime and flame, sustain us   with these sharp tricks of flavour

make do, make do   until the fattening

of the light

In 2020 we held on

these days when the eye of the world
droops nearly closed, nictating milk-light

these days when the skin opaques
stretched thin over the rattle, barely containing the pip

these days when the embers of seeds
can't fall far enough from the branch to even think about growing

these days when the earth licks away
the scrapes of machines, revives the microbe armies

these days when we hold each other drowning
in the choppy wake of our dwindling water

these days when we talk and talk
and talk until tongues fork from trying to mean

these days when we tilt our heads giddy and can't recall
what we spent every hour worried about

these days when everyone is made of knives

these days when the empty sky reflects
only single trees, evenly spaced, standing dead still

Some things are true

There are nights you don't see them. A spine curves
like the earth, the head goes with it. I know you're thinking *I'm nothing*
like a globe, but I don't mean the lies we're told—so storied
in the bone that the same blue marble flashed up in a bunch of skulls
right then—how animated we feel by what we know
we know. Bulb after bulb, starburst after star,
burst. I mean the truth. This world was never perfect
in its roundness, her back, too, is fallen in. The *s* is somewhere
in the sea, and every wave that ever breaks sounds out
that shape, the way it hurts. The ocean breathes
through her teeth. I make a sound just like her when the stars
fill my eyes, escape my mouth. When the head falls back at last
ungravitied from days of trying to focus on every
instrument at once. If we're lucky, it's a clear night. If we're lucky,
we breathe out until morning. Then, we do it again. Wipe the pane
clean and you'll see them. Not one thing round—shattered pop
and sizzle. Static, wave, and burst. Drink the lie of lumen
with unshuttered eyes. Take it, take it in right
from the source.

Ocean circus

Your ticket is torn by opening
your eyes. The ragged flap of the wind

cannot shut out hawking sky, selling sugar-
churned clouds licked to shape

by hill tongues. This coast greedy, all the waves' hours
tumblers perform – the music of bodies

in motion, pebbling defiant applause. And at curtain,
all of it sand. Unmountains. Hard glitter.

In the limn

I have swum out deep. The only sound
is the bow-wave moltening away

from my hands, folding tonguelesss
phonemes. I'll never capture that lilt

in our language of unliquid, of hard
mouth shapes. I fear I'll never capture

many things. I am strongest
stroking somewhere between breast

and crawl, and to everything that belongs
out here surely I'm the thing caught

between states. Not swimmer, not floater.
Pushed upward by water, weighed down

by air, no longer fish but still wearing
the shapes of fins as he lurches terribly

along, and quite unable
to stay dry – look at him, always leaking

something. There's a colour that hums
between blue and green. You never see it anywhere

but right here, looking down
through the glass and miles from everywhere.

It's neither, it's both. It fills you up
to the gills with peculiar

desire – to blur the line there
until you've no clue which way is up.

Feeding the koi

You save the crusts from the good brown loaf,
not truly stale, but tired. On your early walk

through the city gardens, there is a patient round mirror
to crumble them into, and in it an unfamiliar creature,

folded and loose in his aspect. He watches you from the water.
You have never met his eyes, although you sense they are kind.

This morning, autumn has nodded last orders at the trees
and the ember of the squalling sun catches

a plume at his throat, and his blur blushes bright — young
with reborn flame. In the dry world the wind arrives

to spread the blaze outward in ripples
from the man standing, the man lying, with his hands full

of burning bread, and when the fish surface
their mouths make round holes in his body.

In one tiny circle after another the fire
goes out. Cool water —O O O—

welling dark and smooth
from the gut. It was always the truth.

What feeds on us that steals our fire.
What we feed to remember what we are.

Coeliac bird god

She jokes that I'm some kind of deity
to sparrows. Every morning, manna
flows from the back door to the feeder
via this two-legged conduit. I don't tell her
that a self-made god does this kind of thing
at least a little selfishly. To fend off a life-
long struggle with purpose. The certainty
I breathe for any reason in particular
has escaped me, and this body is not godly
in any way that matters, struggling too
in its ridiculous ways – simple bread
an indigestable substance, even a crumb
slow poison to it. Forever hungry
and jealous and clearly no transubstantiation
will happen in this temple. And yet,
barely awake, I find my hands again full
of stale risk and crusts of purpose, a heel
of godhood, dangerous only to me.
Take a step back. Another. The door
is barely shut and pale flames alight
to consume the feeder in a flickering miracle
of birdy fire. Offering accepted, gone,
and in the glow of it I wonder
who's really blessing whom. I can't blame
anything exotic for the warmth inside,
we're too far south for mythic wicks
of waxwings, far too damp
for a phoenix. Sparrow paradise must be noisy
and strangely polite, the way they queue
for their chance at the bounty. I hope

a bird god doesn't need to eat. I hope
a bird god has no purpose at all
except to carry bread. I hope for morning,
at times like this when my hands clench
completely empty in the dark. She sighs
in her sleep, the tail of exhale
a whistle, a chirp. Tomorrow I hope
to feed something until it's full.
God, or not.

Walking in willing

One night you'll take your feet, grown soft and cold, to the river.
Old ferns throw their monster's shadows there, fit to loom a body
small within its skin. Night's water ripples restless – full of eyeless
eels, dripped streaks of pale milk, a queasy light to yaw you to the
runway. The candle-road you'll find to follow goes where trees are
lured unkind (even to one another). Persist. Push through thick
arguments of thorn and scrape and bleeding bark – the house plays
hide-and-seek. You'll know you're close when burning sugar sours
the wind, when you're scared by song and breathing in spent smoke
of wishes always better than the cake. You'll know you're warmer
still when tiny bones of ghosts float in, flash constellations in the ink
a fish, a mouse, a cat, the game, oh all the games long lost. And there's the
door – wide open now, and yes it always was. The house alone knows
just how tight you've closed your eyes for years, the clagging fear
that's sealed you shut. And you will run that endless hall, barefoot and
half your size, you snarl of creature wordless all your worth and
weight unwound you tear the ugly curtains down from every room.
There in that place the dusty, streaming light, it can remake a skin so
smooth, so bold, new page.

There's not a myth or terror-tale on earth that hasn't been retold a
thousand ways. That house where you're afraid to live? It will be
eaten by the woods.

Keep this story by your bed. The quickening pulse inside your walls
is reading it aloud, and dying

to believe it, even now.

In these moments

Roots take the shape of their container,
bound by how they began. And still what grows up

and out from there is all its own – a plant
in tight square shoes opens leaves

as the hands of a supplicant, fingers spread
to receive the manna of the light. You might say oh

but that's in the hum of the seed, I say we sing
ourselves beyond the plans of these bodies.

And really isn't any plan just a bargain
between a beast and Chronos – we ink our water

with intent to stay the course, and hope that means
he holds the dust and lets us sail. No harvest

until we're done. We seldom win that bet.
Well, I unplan these bones, I am throwing all that

to the wild. The pots are smashed, the shoes
are lost, my hungry leaves

are opening all at once. The world I am is tired
of holding steady and the world

beyond this skin is tired. What I'm sure about
is this honey rain of light, every second

waiting to be eaten. What I'm sure about
is your eyes on me – that look you get, up-

tilted as a newly-watered thing, still growing
until it can't. What I'm sure about

is that we grew so hard we lifted off the roof.
Sun came longing for our shadows –

that dark in us that spills its length, in floods
beyond this dirt.

Baltic amber

One bead, singing warmth – small palmed weight
gravid with 44 million years

My eye strokes the long blink of a slow life, tender
tastings of long-gone light
eaten into yourself by open-mouthed leaves

your blood, honey   your feet, divining water
        your crown, greened
     by a young and frivolous sun

All the time in the world
to play a forest
down to its glow

Action/potential

The first room you entered here
was lightless. Wet spring, still wound, you would-be-

bud – first test: your will to leave the heavy press
of dark. And you prevailed and won

the map – like this, each seedling learns to read
which way is up, right as the here-be-dragons

of the blueprint start to stir within the vein, to roar
your wild awaits outside

all compass and container. And once I climbed
a greenhouse just to feel

what it was to walk away from everything
on nothing, and when I fell right

through the glass I landed on another waning
interest gone to dust. A body left waiting

in the dim for years, pale yellow shoot
strained out to tongue the graze

of sunlight seeping through the filthy panes. Split
plastic pot, hard dirt, she was a thirsty snarl of bone-

white roots, packed solid to conform. I left her there –
I'd not grown real enough to yet conceive

of what I could or couldn't save, and summer
and her promises, they beckon a bleeding child on, away,

away from every kind of broken house. But little did I know
the weather a chance lets in, what was cracking

in my wake – that even though the soil begins to dry
when watering first becomes a bind, a slip can break you

open to the rain. And little did they know
how long a shoot can wait to see the sky

fall in, even told its roots go nowhere
good. The lie: there's a window

of time for taking hold, then the window shuts
forever. The truth: you can walk out on the glass.

The dare: Walk out when you're sure
the glass will not support your weight.

The Engine

Travelling light

At the end of that road, a sanctuary
for endangered birds. One room kept in darkness,
housing unmooned hunters. Ghosts-in-waiting, painting flight
on our pinpricked arms. Dust, drifting.

At the end of that road, a carillion, blank sockets
dangling rotted ropes, the only sound left swelling there
the struck pewter bell of the sea. We stole back hours, drowned
all doubt, sang loud with the thump of the tyres. Kited our hearts.

At the end of that road was another road, narrowing twists
that lead to a hill track that wisped to a trail of iron sand trickled
from a loose fist spilled to the south wind. Your hair
her own creature, waving cursive. Long clouds signed you like a letter.

And that one road led to the airport, a circle
for which we were not prepared, even knowing time moves
in her way like a human child, arms out, spinning to test
the balance. Giddy on takeoff, and the sun rose with no warning

that at the end of the road, every wheel finds friction
to turn its imprint. That all our travelling is prayer, that I'd find you
left in the narrows and as birded dark, pocketing the wind and named
by nimbus and singing out the window along the coast:

save me, save me, save me

that all those roads ahead, sick hairpin we couldn't see, the gridlock
just waiting to seize, they all led here. To your call from the wreckage
of a crushed country, all exits missed, and needing my voice

from the future. To tell you the map stays marked, your pin
left a hole, and next time *–Te Rerenga Wairua–*
we'll be travelling light, so there'll be time for that road
that goes all the way north. I tell you we'll drive just as fast as we can,
as fast as we can away from the cliffs.

Te Rerenga Wairua is a place at the northernmost tip of Aotearoa. Its
name means *the leaping-off place of spirits.*

Commute with the birds

Morning is a step into a cage – these crowds are made of birds
who should have flown. We flock aboard a northbound train

to move these bodies made to move themselves – deny each day
the hollow light inside our bones. We fell into this, all species here;

pin-pinioned town-crows in blackdrip raincoats, crooked
encroachments of elbows, heroned angles

in the ribs – umbrella beaks jab a knee
out of line. The window clatters pigeons, greywing

roof tiles rising from houses. They seem escaped, but they roost
as tight as teeth, then overhead wires

cheesecut their flight to death. Even the crowded air of this city
is a maze, even hedges snarl at each other

over borders – all leaf-memory
of crown-shyness lost. Where are their nesting forests

for their trunks still neighboured snug, yet blue rivers of sky
mapped around their outstretched hands, where one thing sheltering

respects the canopy of another. And from a different train
a lost morning snipped a glimpse of starlings

on the pier in their thousands, still spacing
themselves a möbius of flight, and not one was drowned

by the draft of their launch. I have missed
my stop, remembering how

a single gannet will unpress from the colony, soar miles to fish alone.
Thrown dart of a body, spiralled tight with purpose, beak first

to the water. Oh singular, oh greedy, oh fed by falling
over and over from one world to another.

Root codes

How the canopy sines as a leaf-sea, and the sacrifice
of that one young yew to the wind left a stump.

How a boy was unable to navigate the chop
of the waves that never stopped moving his horizon.

How they were waving flags across three oceans
and the old crests drowned where seas lose their names.

How the network of roots, tingle-fine wiring, carried
the currents of need, and the truncated was fed.

How the synapses are every desire, and signal
when they too are dying, a teenage brain tapping out.

How they remembered that it hurt, to be young
body already unpathed from the map of two flat planes.

How a broken tree greens here unseen, and the whole forest
keeps pumping the message that yew is still yew.

How he rode the invisible wind, how every wire sang
as he translated his fibres through them.

How they opened their hands as soft blue lights in the night
and caught his drift. How his wrong spin was right.

How they are meshed, tangled below the ground.
How they are meshed, tangled beyond their screens.

Microcosm

Night slews in, slowdark inks the pond
    Hine-nui-te-pō's fingers stir giddy a constellation
        of gentled waterbeetles

        In twitching orbit, podfoil bodies surf
    swells of silver equations, arrayed
antennae quivering for any edges to the endless

    Even the wingless will fling themselves at new suns
        jetting vapour at dawn
            to escape this steady drowning

Taniwha country

Unwelcome   old salt-breath rasps
up through my soles   jigging sand eager
to vanish my footed mandalas from his skin

The sea-monster is cranky today, peninsula
of fallen body hunched, slopes steeped
to petulance – the message in earthquakes is
lie down still
with your flea body pressed to his rumbling belly
you remember best – to be alive
is to stay constantly unsettled

The 1930's vivisected a pass
through one shoulder, a wound
held open for traffic. The V bleeds
me back down to the sea   *unwelcome*
unwelcome   here the wind
never whispers or whistles it howls
raw in the bone always
we made quite sure of that

When you say things like this, they call you a bleeding heart

Rounding bitemark bay, the sea gnashes and the rage eye oranging
the horizon lasers the houses   *unwelcome*   all
the cars go first, thrown toys jangling music
and the great scaly beast   oh yeah he's done playing

The wave's shadow is a monstrous claw
and weren't we always parasites waiting
to be scratched
I open my chest to laughing   *welcome*
that wet heart bursts the surf red
with everything I have
ever taken, returned

Fallback (throwback)

Clifftop rocks, sharped by southerlies
      bruise my brave, bared winterings-over

A pretty wind insists my hair to kitestrings, toes scatter
      small scree, bouncing lust for the fall

into the farbelow bay – once caldera, now again
      eager cradle, rocking full of soft blanket-blue

call to the void, you said, but I hear only gulls, urging   *oh, go, go*
    one   more   step   and gravity loosens   her fist

I unravel – apeswing, quickening shrew, nothing
    but open gills   falling back to the breathing water

No (thing is) right

Who told this calm day
it had any right
to reel delicate and radiant
when I am dissolving hard

Who said
that when a person falls
to pieces, there must be noise –
screaming, sharp edges

The only sounds here are distant:
the quiet, ordinary tide
and a long, soft keening –
the wounded ape in me
calling, calling

Lost in the empire

Moon, shut up in her box
of sawn-off clouds. Tapestry
of stone road, unpicked by rip-
root yew. Floating dust, a sneeze
of light, look sharp, torn stitches waiting
to trip you. There's nothing here
that isn't the result of disassembling.
I am dissembling, I keep trying
to break the compass –
to get lost in the cogs of any place
I might find myself making tracks.
In the kind of forest that's best
for confusing yourself, there are slabs
of shadow, a bread too dense
for modern trees suckling
our frailing sun. This kind of dark
buttered its claim in each wraith
of hedgerow two thousand years gone.
To set foot now, lost boy, is to kick
at jaws never unclenched
since the take, not even
for a minute. What does that do
to a spirit whose meat unchose the fight,
bitten into the dirt by iron
and blood and root – I ask you
how hungry must a ghost be
with not one mote to manifest? Get lost
just enough, they say it rattles the moon
in her box, bleeds her worry, like a mother's,

through the cracks. Enough silver
to fill the solemn cup
of a hand. I'm starting to think I could crouch here
and pour for years – feed the dark everything I am
and still not see anything like a man
made solid enough to find his way back.

Statistics

Runners find bodies. We don't talk
about it, but it haunts miles in advance.

I'm the kind who follows
his feet. They remember the time

when they were fins – it's right there
in the bone. The way they swim

this shadow sleeker than the shape I am
turning currents in the silk-cool air

of an early morning trail. An old sea left her dead
beneath my sweep – shells are gritted teeth. A sea

never follows a path – creatures washed deep
into trench-roots and leaf-dark. Ghost pincers nip

my heels, calves, thighs. *Don't trip. Don't crush*
anything human. Would I know if I did.

In 1987 we flew to arcturus in a box labelled 'roofing nails'

All the doors are closed and what we build we secure

with long pins. My house, yours, stuck

through the belly, supposed dead on the board. Listen,

at night, like your guts depend on it – something like dreams still

oozes from the hole in the shell. Quietly, stone bangs against stone,

determined to summon the mountain, the molten summers

of childhood. In the rough isobars of four-by-two, there's weather

sheared clean, pine still muttering about the cone.

What kind of afterlife is it to see everything

you must protect contain itself, admiring the shine

of each nail knocked into the dark crate. *Beetle, beetle, break the glass.*

A cardboard box will do. Take this ship to the stars.

Hathor's gift

Last night you called me from the bottom of a well
and I pictured the signal between us as a rope ladder
woven from a bunch of old strings attached. A bit frayed,
this connection, and this analogy, but both holding together
just enough for you to see the ladder a little bit more clearly
than you were seeing the rope. And I don't care if we've not spoken
since before the world cracked its lid, I'm just grateful
I still look like some kind of stick when the alligators
find the ass. So often it's hard to respect the tree
in someone who's fallen
in an indifferent swamp, over and over, they think
the fall makes you soft wood. But it was you who told me Hathor
kicked out the crocodile god even though she was
at least partly a cow. I bet they underestimated just how fierce
a prey animal waxes when her herd is in the dark
and feeling the closing teeth. I bet they underestimated her
even after she teamed up with the sun itself
and gored the darkness threatening her loved ones on the tips
of her kind, soft horns. Stabbed it until it was striped
with secondhand light, then drowned it
in her milk of most inhuman kindness.

I mean how do we balance at all

At centre you carry the weight / I don't mean
a heart but yes chambers liquid
with iron / I don't mean blood I mean
restless and betrayed only by being
magnetic / your core invisible
to something on the surface
otherwise / I mean a heart is a constant kind
of collision / I mean momentum
dizzies us / sure as a slow leak
in the moon. I mean we tide.
I mean our being off-
balance has flow-
on effects. I don't mean
to be dense / I mean if your heart
was different this whole life thing
would collapse. I mean fragile.
I mean, it is.

Black hole primer

Spiralling was the best game, kids testing
what it is to be a bone-caged brain –
on the green sky of the lawn we'd collapse, done
whirling, all the meat of a small body
impacting on itself, sloshed giddy into spinning black
behind closed eyes

After falling, I used to pretend I was still
falling
down through the queasy earth, folded
into a different animal

The heatwave summer killed the lawn, and we compressed
into adulthood, spiralling only debts and wound
tighter and tighter until all the spring
left us

So if we go down now, spun into ourselves
let it be like it was –
rationality fled, dizzy
marvel at discovering
this thing at our core. Look. You always held a ticket
back into the spangled dark

At Pariwhero (Red Rocks)

Night cay   crag coast   gale force   seal colony

shale rock   delicate boy   no coat   empty bottle

flung shatter

picked glass   tender weapon   precipice, precipice,

precipice

no warning   every warning   life flow   cold sea

strobe light   wave shock   real surprise, how much fight

there is left   ink quiet

if this was a story the selkies would save him

if this was a story there'd be a magical coat

if this was a story the coat would be found

the next day – far from this place and still just as empty

of boy

as it was, but pockets full of certain,

not stones. *Transformed*, we'd nod, with the sudden wisdom

of someone handed a map – all the horror

sunk. *Never meant*

for this world. Swimming his bleeding heart out.

Act like you were never for sale

On those days we were flutter and varnish. Time blown
on the tradewinds — toys for the updraft, downdraft, too hard

and brittle-bright for any landing but the spurt and gasp
of applause. And on those days we painted the unspeakable

feelings, the ones that never made it
into the script, on hot ripe faces with palmed-

palm-sugar and unguent-of-anthers, and on those days
those same faces slipslid their gaudied eyes and touched their cheeks

together intimately, brief and baked electric with proper unsaids,
and on and on arced those spat-out days

when the electric that moved us
moved us wet with big colour in that little pond

of footlights all thrashing *pick me* from the swirl
of young eels, him so slender, her good

bright needle-teeth, and on those days *company* meant
only that we played together well, that even

the most badly bitten didn't drop
a word or miss a step, or when they did the faces they'd loved-by-

painting bled laughter tainted kindly, and not yet
like they smelled a life dripping away

into the water or as if they'd finally bumped
against the glass, seen

the strings of our dangling tags, and some of that last part
is a lie. But who doesn't want to lie just as pretty

as something made to end up in a prettier box, for now
sticky with the ghosts of fertile anthers, and so we bite

into recall again and again, this cake now
invisible on the pink plastic

saucer so sweet, so sweet and falling to bits
in the grass. And these days we know the magic

poured out of that flimsy doll's teapot, it's more real
than you've been in your life. Don't ever act

like it didn't —like it doesn't—
make you sick.

Unstuck

What kind of night is best,
I ask the mouse,
for a harvest? The stars
were supposed to know
but they stopped speaking to us
when our unsleeping cities
shouted them down. From space
we must be a constant howl. Why
would anything keep raising
its voice. I'm not sure how far I ran
or who was more surprised
to find a warm parcel of pulse out here
wrapped tight against the engine
of his breath. But his fur makes jewels
of my question, condensed
to something real and delicate
for him to carry. I feel it leave me, the quick oil
of him flows the race of thorns, cogs born
to tick the forage. I will lie down
in the weeds, tell him everything
I'm still so hungry
to say before I go. Watch
the deft weave of his gathering
wipe free all my want
on the poke of many needles
that never touch him once.

Extinction event

They left no bodies
        that morning. Vision-pigeons suffocate
without fuss, dociled
        by so many tablets – that
spackling, neatened into the cracks
of a birded boy

Still, where their small corpses weren't, nobody
        trod – slippers slipping around
cold not-feathers sticking
        to the linoleum days

of doses, mouthchecks forced
        dragoning at the gone sun
cherry eyes, rolling tongue sevens
        the right combo meaning
they said   successful treatment   I said
        oh, loss.

When it happens, the quiet is upsplit earth
        gone to rift
the clear-eyed bell of unblackbird's call, done
        his spell tongue glazing tile
to white morning
        sky, no more hungry
shower curtain pattern warbling panicsong

So here is your order, then, this lack of body, this
tidy clean wax stopping my ears, here
is my functioning – a dead-eye membrane, smalled
wilting through the rest of ordinary time

How lucky then, to have seen the tangled strings –
tugging up creatures, busy
living away hard with no clue
that when they can't hear or see you   you no longer exist

The Blockage

Letting lie

Leave the soft grass fringe
unbrushed from meadows' eyes
and watch the humming thumbs of bees
sweep tender the skin of the earth.
How they trace her freckle daisies
left rampant in the sun. And when the sun and bees
are done, allow the trees, their leaves
that ate up sugar-light, to drift their fill of crisp.
In layered calmness round their feet, the soil sweets.
All this magic that we hold.
All done by holding back.

Last chance to settle

On this long shard, we tiltwalk our builds and burials.
Even low ground here is eyrie, each rock the poke
of sea-hid volcanoes – every scaffold

is a drowning. Squid-haunted rebar, whale-groaned cellars, ghostwater
of the Eocene – most of an island is a body trailing below a flood.
Our small dry bones

are surface detail, the very oldest shallow-shook in hot iron sand, tapu
just seven scant centuries. The sea unsacreds us easily, all
our smooths and roughs, our clingings-on

to barely-unmolten peaks – wild teeth that cut bite early, fanging
the bright thin air above the sweet broad plate of
Gondwanamama, easier geographies still unweaned. And we,

we hungry water-skimmers, we skeletons-in-waiting – left her alone
straining barely above the aching blue. When finally we landed
so late, so heavy

on this last unfooted earth, how she trembled, now
how she holds her breath.

Wellington airport is built on reclaimed land

We rode horses here
Her words pace quietly, landing crescents
in the spaces between jet-engines. Our own feet touch

down the beach with no sound. Sand enough left
for four soft shoes, chasing the crisping of hooves
across once-were-dunes. She walks with her eyes closed

fragile lids shutters for seven decades gone, runway
all run away, simpled to daisy-trails
before this island waxed international, and the southerly

is bitter, flinging kerosene. Still, one of us breathes
sun-dusted crabgrass and sweet manure.
I drive her back in silence, willing

her lungs buoyant-full of that child summer, for her sleep
tonight, and oh please for a few more years yet.
At dark, I return. Sit watching

the black race of the bay, the reflections
of tail-lights. How they prance
over the water.

Ice

An afternoon tantrum of hail
follows rain's deafening argument.

The Esplanade lies stunned white
under icebergs, unseasoned

and embarrassed by such public fury.
In their million-dollar

seafront houses, the occupants
are also embarrassed – rage-

weather reveals you
here *in paradise* – stormdrain rats unsecret

themselves. These once-sailor rodents are canny
to floods, a century and a half settled in

lessons to flee rising water – driven wet
-nest-rockets. But hail doesn't happen here, not here

in *the tropics* we don't like to think
about the ice; cold, pale, suddenly here. Glossied

by the brazen bruise-
light sky, missiled bodies lie fat in the street.

The ice-sheets, already melting,
will drift them home to dark tunnels,

so in the evening it's an easy jog up the hill, nothing
on the road but the painted blue line

and the stylised wave, meaning
Tsunami-safe-zone. From the ridge, a stain

of roofshadow creeps the battered beach, longing
toward the drains. Come bullroarer wind

rolling memory on its tongue – pūrerehua shivers
the hairs, prickled cloud breathes out a clock

of moon, hands of light pulling up wave
after wave and she never stopped

ticking – one minute
you're running with your kids

to higher ground. The next,
the sky will be falling.

Oceanography

Bird-mapped, the river tributaries
that nourished her
are the veined caul of a wet body

The hugeness of a placental lake
drying at the edges, still
desperate to feed

In the tidal flats, the blood slows
salt-silted, heavied with proximity
to her five deep hearts

Just keep telling yourself
there was no incubator
ready for this emergency

Small blue love –
it is the most terrible thing, to see the infant
in someone who is losing the fight

Gullible eggs

My mother laid small lies
to toughen the shells
of her gullible eggs

I believed with all my yolk
she was a whole century wise
an alien, herself
hatched from stars
when the world was black and white

When stories crack
so do we, leaking out
the whole of childhood

Take two (2) in the morning, after disclosing as needed (i.)

The medicine I drip… dripped into you was my own discovery
    —this is how you save a life when you're both six—
One leaf shrined from autumn, yellow siren
loud, calling the tongue
to lick a prayer, synapses sherbetting, buds on hard fizz
    —burn from your mouth those words—
Two roadrunners escape through a rose-garden.
Philtre-whispers fill your ear on the hoof: this secret I know
is the biggest
    —it did not loom like yours or mine but oh I wanted it to block out the sun—
Did you know, every colour tastes different
    —anticipation adrenalined you back to life behind your eyes—

Methodical of jaw, we ate our way around the hybrid teas, sampled
floribunda, ramblers. Rules laid down obvious; a single bite
from each, then judgement:
one careful, perfect close of teeth
    —proud-lost incisor, you had to tilt your head
like you were always asking a question, for any decent closure—
around the quivering heart (so red, gold, white as a lie), leaving each
bloom neatly gutted
    —this is what "love" is—
Your winner was strawberry-pink, delicate as a
    —Secret-Rosa, Rosa-Secret—
I spat icebergs, you strained
someone else's laugh through pulped crimson, and I would never tell
you about the bitter
worm I chewed that day and quietly
oh so quietly swallowed whole.

берёзы
(Birch trees)

All sound that is not crows is forgotten – forever

has passed. The blank-bellied sky is torn open

by black warnings – beaks, trees – bleeding fat snow.

No bell of colour marks an hour, a leaf, a fingertip, the march

of trees trudges as I do, a scar between

       white earth,   white air.

In this place, on the echo of this day, they sang sap-rush

into the birches

the white goat stamped back the spring, shook

ancient winters from her horns

but my tongue took no northsongs with its milk – Mother Russia

smooths my heartbeat quiet   slow   *silent*

her feast-day given to crows.

Sea gods self-soothe

Tangaroa's belly flattens, swells
into the bright blade. Light honed by a creeping moon
is the sharpest of all light, slipped glass

ruptures him – quickening mercury
beads through cold ink. At his edges, silvered

waves break, and break
again –this, love, is the very nature of waves–

but to shush, shush yourself calm, knowing
the shattering will go on until even the moon is dust, this

only gods should have to do

Group therapy for clever crabs

There were no windows and we spoke of home
as therapy – those who had tongues
not yet unhooked by their dosage

Mrs Jesus sang, predictably
–Ave, ave, the roasting flare of the sacred heart the warmest hearth– her rosary
chattering DT-teeth in time with our rolling eyes

Quiet Joni said nothing, but beyond her starved-skull-smile a hatbox
spiralled out coloured scarves in the wind of a Julie-Andrews
meadow, popping daisies

Simon, lion-posed on his chair, just roared
for the fortieth time that morning, his teacup bounced steel drums,
greening-gold, Zion's royal spires and he o king of crowds

And the nurse foghorned on – what about family, what about
people and houses and such
things that are normal like windows and loved ones and gardens, until
my faraway reason-voice came as thrown grey paint – *please understand,
we are only crabs*

And I could not say this then: when the weight
of the world cracks your careful shell
the pink cringe of a person
finds whatever it needs to mean safety – a rusty can a palace
when everything else has been thrown away

Glacial body

Under magnification, human bone alive
is skimmed aurora, and the fracture a cliff
of wind-cut ice. To snap up the blue hum
of a glacier, the human eye crackles focus
and there we lie, glow laid bare to the aeon-blade
flensed of our cushion dirt. The owner of this bone
will survive the moraine, fallen deep
to the chill dark of chemical sleep, while the rill of his pulse
quivers that brutal cliff and complicates the fix
and in the dark the ice too is moving to the wiles
of its own slow will, vitals steady.
We think it unconscious. We think it dead.
They say I am lucky to shiver awake, but luck would mean forgetting
old bones have no colour at all – lost airless, pressed lightless.

This poem did not stand a chance

Begotten, I failed to thrive, all at once
and for years after, perhaps

> *this poem will be rejected*
> *before it can speak*

from spite. I learned young that
every strand and bead of us is base, self-
interested only in making more
of itself

> *this poem will know it can never be*
> *good enough*

Here is a sore-tooth socket of a truth for a tongue to test –
we persist by errors
in our replication, success
for this whole bolt of shivering animal fabric
is in the dropped stitches, in failing
to be perfect

> *this poem will blame itself*
> *for signalling predators*

this also describes a number of fathers;
selfish patterns unstrung, then unshuttled, lacking
any binding, so

> *this poem will unravel red threads*
> *into the sea*

> *this poem will fail to finish*
> *even that*

I have stopped you going on. I did not
beget, I have not made anything at all of myself

> *this poem*
> *was stillborn*

I pick up this small body
of work, headed for the coffin-drawer, and it is still
warm and so

blameless

a great rack-and-rattle shakes the mistake of it from my hands, even
despite resurrecting you, it begins to speak:

this poem was still
born

Ghost Song

(titled after The Doors song of the same name)

At the world's edge, two figures, frozen
on the lip. Night-jasmine creeps the cliff, wilding

galactic – stabbed stars, vibrating voidwind.
And the taut dark heaves, and splits
in two – some change too huge for skin to bear. *Some god laughed*

us into being, I think you said, *some god who belonged to no-one.*
But the vines have eagered
through the gap now, and I climb their offering-road

to the altar out of time. Your shining face all ripe awe, beloved,
a milkflash moon below. When next you tip over the edge

of 1am, just know you once saw it all *–impossible–*
and the only-ever truth.

Urban plan

When it dawns you are a city
it's a heavy responsibility. In your streets
everyone is hungry all the time, eating
of your dust. I read that skin flakes are, to a mite,
something like a bowl of cornflakes. After breakfast,
I will the behemoth to its feet, an earthquake
of indecision, my somewheres sounding tiny sirens.
Should I warn them about this latest inevitable change
of climate, what will befall us all
when I subside into the sea, one flawed brick
at a time? It might be easier on everyone
not to see it coming. I've run along the crumbly edge
of these cliffs so many times, matter-of-fact
that rocks bounce free, that soles slip
of their own accord. There's never been any plan
except to finally reach the wide field beyond
the walls, to sink down into grass so cool, so sweet,
everything you carry leaps to feed it.

Watershed (Scorpio sun/Scorpio moon)

Star-crone, she named herself, in her stories of back-whenever.
Twitching the thrown bones of her fingers, describing
conducted constellations, the sky whimsy music,
her own fertility orchestra.

Womb on the downhill, she hexed it with charts,
back to a cupped-handclap genesis:
two nasty ragboy remnants evicted,
all pink flashing vacancy (clean rooms) for that coveted girl.

She lies a great deal, but I've no doubt she planned this.
The curled shrimp of my coracle launched precisely
on Pluto's shadow-sea, each suck filling
her witch-child's chambers with dark water, darker.

But she didn't plan on the moon, she who colluded with
my Scorpion brother, she didn't plan on
his ten-cent firecracker midwifing sudden labour
mid-Guy Fawkes-party – any wonder I was a revolt.

The moon loves a good joke at our expense.

Unable to laugh, her creepy-crawly kid floated in
twice-flooded, and his (!)
sting swollen with disgusting empathy
useless for all potions except one.

Her hands shake these days with something that isn't power.
My sponge of a moon swirls tenderness at her shrinking, I dose
her tea with my honey-venom,
and I tell her over and over
how glorious, how mighty
the sorceress you were.

The Gift

You never asked what happened
to your favourite mug. On my way to the ocean
I walk past the home for the elderly around the corner
from where I now live. Me, this unanticipated adult.
With these unscheduled steps.
Sometimes I look up
at the little bubbles of convex windows, angled
to catch the last of the sunlight. Treated to rainbows.
The last we spoke I was fourteen
and you were alive and I was barely.
The last word you said to me was 'anything'.
One of those windows heard anything you spoke last
of all. I smashed that mug on purpose, and I took the bits
to the ocean and I fed them to the sea. She swallowed them
without a sound – broken pieces
far too small to make a splash.
Decades in the dark change a thing.
This fragment of tidegift blue in my palm is heavy
and has no sharp edges at all.

Book/marks
(for S)

Twelve years ago, you left
(me)

your book of sea-poems –
tonight, in a secret
pillow-moon of lamplight
I untuck the dogear on page 4
tender as a shaming
never teased

The gone-shape of your hand
moves counter to mine
and regret folds me clean in half –
that the creases we leave behind
are so easily unfolded

On the day they burned you
I filled your cold palm
with tiny shells
tucked closed the fingers
that had already marked this page

for later

Interactions in (un)controlled conditions

Here is the boy who once caused Chernobyl
to be known as terror-not-town.
It was singlehanded and he was just fifteen
years of slow meltdown, design-flaws, all
his wrong secret buttons pushed in sly dark – a child
who first heard the word delusion as an echo
down a hot tunnel of dissolving ground.

The concrete sarcophagus for his containment
was ugly, poured in the frightened 1970s
to conceal runaway reactions from the general populace
until they safely (oh privately, quietly please) exhausted themselves.

Inside, he found several alien suns still glowing, right
where the lino in the back corridor was scorched, a blast-map
orbited by squeakshoe nurses (15 minute check!), and in that universe
each 2am LadyJesus flamed hard with belief, postal-slot of breast
flapped up. On Sundays she wept Latin and milk, baptised
him in the night-bulb glow
of her earnest sacred heart. He thanked her

with the only language he had available – invocations
of formulae, streaming
ionising radiations from his med-leadened tongue –
cooling rods falling, failing, fast.

On his 16th birthday Joni Mitchell (not her real name)
baked him a cake in a mug, oatmeal
and grated music, she was
57 years of daisychain waterfall

skirts so proud of her matching
57 pounds and counting
down and she watched
his chewing mouth like he was
all the sunsets she'd missed in there.

Digesting, no-strings, you begin to forget
how poisoned your skies are.

Simon was no-one else but Simon,
the most ginger Rasta, Jah Simon, Jah you
beauty, with your redemption songs
expanding the sad showerblock to livity, then
suddenly Simon was no-one at all
–15 minute check!– except that one
time enough for a terrycloth ladder to Zion.
His family had never visited
but they sued.

A huge red lion stalked the ward for weeks.

The whole place burned down last month, a new
banged-up mind went critical, I wondered
who, and what remained of that kid
whose very fabric had knitted delusion all round him for comfort
where the world's nets failed – all the catchers unsafe, not
Mrs Jesus or Joni,
not trustworthy, hunted lions,
and to deserve the rest, his core
knew he must have done something so evil
it melted the innocence from a whole town
10,000 miles away from here.

I don't miss being a nuclear disaster,
but sometimes, in the black smoke of 2am,
float lost prayers, petals of song, distant roars,
and in the slag of all our lives,
I miss the way it made complete sense
of the damage.

Gullible eggs (reprise)

My mother lied with tenderness, sweet
aplomb, and range;
she'd seen a century, our crooked sea-swelled house
cost a million, and all babies were born with feathers
that softened the world's edges.

She blew drifts of invisible down from my cochlea
eased fine barbs from my eyes
and just like that I could see them, settling around me.
But you, my chickadee, are special, she said, *it is clear,*
as I conducted flurries, hearing snowbird music.

In my secret tunnels behind the grazing toetoe, the voice
popped fricatives, blistering the skin
of the ground to open, speaking wounds.
The tidewrack treehut quaked, strobe-boom-
sand-shiver, leaves a hurting kind of green. Not quickly enough
I learned my human friends did not have ancient mothers
who had plucked them free of birth-fluff in their nests.

No bird can keep a secret, and my own cuts became too loud,
perhaps when I autopsied the sea (she is dying) to better hear
the crystal chime of her teeth, rimed blue with salt and festooned
with seaweed tripes, they fished me up
and I woke head netted, deepsea-phosphorescent with electric dots,
stinking of burning
eider. And wet and singed I learned
to lie – almost as well as my mother.

She's two decades shy of a hundred, and all those tilting seaside-huts
do now cost a million or even more, and I tell her
I'm okay and it's true and not-true, but when the world speaks
in blizzards, I catch every feather, lay them
opaque upon her eyes, puff cumulus to spiral her eardrums.

For you, my mummer-bird, are special – that was always clear, and now
the truth. Now it's the time for soft edges.

Berlin's *Memorial to Homosexuals Persecuted Under Nazism* was last vandalised in August 2019

Beneath the seat the world is reduced to shoes
and I guess at people by their feet, growing whole lives
from soiled leather, a scuffed sandal, a lost aglet – I am not yet five
and the oildirt smell from beneath the floor is bigger
than being lost – I do not know where
we are going or who is driving this train
or where it will stop, but chopped-up light
is breathing colours across my palm –*bright dark bright dark*–
we are streaking through trees, the clever windows (you showed me
how thick, how safe, the emergency exit)
tugging strands of this unknown forest's sun
into a rainbow rope I cannot hold.
I will learn, later
I will see shoes in piles and lives will sprout from them
I will identify
with rainbows and kids whose names
were not sewn into their coats for them to be found.
I will learn about prisms and how
the clear light of day
hides every stripe inside it – trapped triangular, they split hard
and may be picked out one by one
by one, and I am not five
and everywhere trains are now leaving
every second and where are we going and who
is driving
and this time
where will it stop

Manifest

These bodies we sail like the first boats,
knots and all, ignoring the leaks

until they sink us. When we stripped
away the bark and sank the chisel

and saw the rill of rings, the chambers
left by families of owls, the shapes

of organs left us wanting green. So natural
that liverwort's fleshy lobes

would prime the filter, or that a walnut
oiled every tongue and groove

inside the hard wood of a head. That saxifrage
unroots the stones among the beans. And I know

we've died of willingness to believe
in a hand that signs the manifest

more legibly than all our jokes about physicians.
And yet I see the ivy boats, their jute-brown sails

snapping in the wind of a trunk's horizon – eyes slide
to watch our passage from the grain, above

full-throated choirs of leaves. My manifest is scrawled
with names of illnesses that boarded ages back –

new cures are shaped like tiny stones. Some boats
are stabilised by ballast, and some go under

sinking slow
when magic leaves the wood.

Why I didn't look for your stone for fifteen years

In the quiet silver wind
datura's a hardy ghost.
Tendrils black with fleeing light,
trumpets white as the mushroom-
moon, the only movements here.
Whoever planted that vine
in the sorrowing soil by the wall
chose it for the commoner's name:
but no trumpets of angels rip the air
and no salt drips from the clouds
(without, within)
when at last I find you there.
Grey as ashes, hidden well
behind the woody ropes of clamber
dangling sickly lamps – your name,
that Mr._____. It sits uneasy
on my grown-up shoulders now
as it was always going to, and when I brace,
uncling that vine, to be quite sure,
the plant's persistence pulls us free.
What's left – a fading hint of letters.
An absence none can read.

Elegy for two goth teenagers

We grew centimetres in cemeteries. Books
and candles, sans the bell. To sit among the ghosts
is to solid yourself, by comparison. Halfway between the stone
and the spirit – some days the blank-eyed angel. Your features
were inclined towards the sweet, your hands
drawn strong to bitter. The hard paints they found
to chase the human from your face
convinced the mirror. I, so unreflective,
knew you hollow beneath the round, a blown egg
painted black. We edged brittle
around the needle-poke, the cracks. And when you smashed
to bits, they glued you wrong – pillowed on a colour
you'd toddlered. Your cheeks apples, rosy,
long poisoned. I saw you beckon in the worm.

Art history

We argued aesthetics that whole year –
you with gold-dust in your corner, me mooning

over silver. The sighs that left your lips
whenever the lecturer mentioned Zoia

substantiated spangled curls – your gaudy Fibonaccis.
Your opinions sprung the air for days. *Austerity*

they'd tinkle over my preference for Saint Petersburg
in winter, all lunar-and-pale-blue. *Second place.*

And I only smiled gibbous, because the game
was to remain the ghost, to haunt your gilt. We're so needy

of the wind-up, when there's tension that can never spring.
So when you went and split, three days before

that long-awaited trip, I thought you'd simply
struck it rich, embraced the god I knew you were. Ripe-

sprouting corn or wheat somewhere, or suffocating for your art
in a second molten skin.

When I heard you'd succumbed
to quite ordinary water, I was flying over Siberia – hours of nothing

but blinding ice, silverblue and wounded deep with rivers.
The sun arrived like a cough –

loud, and with no thought for breath,
and it turned out you were right the whole time.

Hold the river

You told me you haven't been outside in 57 days
and tonight the river is a dropped ribbon, limp and lost
and the sharp stones of the trail as I begin to run
become the sound of something chewing. The faster
we go, the faster we're eaten. You are moving,
in the lines of your confinement, so slowly now
you have become a painting in my head   —static—
existing not to be touched. And in the guilty, lucky air
down here we're starting up the engines
and on my knees in the soft mud I can hear the first plane
for months, idling beyond the water. I'd wish you were here,
but the wind is whipping up cold, and the coming dark
is frantic with sudden birds, woken startled
from their neat new nests along the runway.

This is not a myth

Everyone knows a good dog
comes when it's called
and hell, I called her, unaware
of the bargain, the leash tightening
everyone's choke. Maybe you'll blame me
for the end of the world
like I do – but last time I said sorry, I tried to tell you
of the falling-pit, no end to the down,
how each 2am's been a howl cramping the chest
for as long as I remember, terror-dried eyes
slammed open to the dark, and each dawn
a bright hurt as the light scrapes in. How many times
did I mouth to the nothing   *take me, just make it all*
stop   *stop*
And out in the blank, something heard. The stars and moon slid gone
as she slunk in, the quiet weather of her mouth exhaled
the hot sours of an ancient cave
and my tired blood leaped alive to promise, to threat
and my toes dead to the earth for days
found the wet rolling hills of her tongue, and so I walked on in.

In her great belly, sleep
like the unspiral of a saved infant, lap-cradled at last.
In her great belly, the picked bones of gods, of all human grief,
names of tears laid to rest.
The prophecy-vault of her ribs has stolen my language of howl,
her hunger piqued
by one modern morsel, for the crunch of continents, to lap up
the sorrowful marrow of the sun.

When she devours you, too, I will find you in the dark.
When I tell you I'm sorry
this time it won't be the truth.

An oral history

The decision slunk in sly
from a field that ate rabbits.

It sniffed out a kitchen, soon
haunted us unfair with howls

(sing, you determined unfed
sing back, you mourning feeders).

This hunger makes a real ass
from a jawbone, weaponed sharp

shape emergent daily
every angle cutting need. A shocking new

mouth. It gives out – but nothing
may enter, even breath

crawls carefully where old meek-tape
is torn, stumbling over unbaby teeth.

And the sickness
that is freefall snarls a nurturer all up

with the orbiting frantic
hollow-boned moonthing

the starveling becomes – dry-white, airless, stuck
in that kitchen far below

and mother-tides roar there in floods
at such new manipulation, breaking

for the days of a child's simple waxing.
Don't we wear our craters well, we

who know all bodies grown of *shut up shut up*
are hungry, hungry still, still howling to forget

that a spine growing hard, pushing up
through tamped-down soil

rips up the family   land

Crepuscular rays on the morning of your surgery

If it takes you, I want it to be like this.
Whet-glass morning on the water,
what just split the old belly
of the clouds out there is a scalpel
as sharp and as silver as the one
tucked up asleep not yet knowing
your name. The well-honed sun knows you
and renames you as she has done
for thirty thousand mornings slipping
her needles of *I am* into the dark
tunnel of your eye, gate just creaking. We flare
back into ourselves each time we crack
the ark. Some days you might need a reminder
that isn't about waking up, but is, and you see
that alchemy on the boardwalk usually
after rain. From the tight grey sheet spills
a streaming, sudden gout
of light. At the slice, all hunch untethers
from a spine, there's a sharpening
of resolve. Someone pauses, bathed
in a squint of bright, then steps on quick:
I am I am I am I am
not even knowing they've been cut.

Why water takes us this way

Come to, still in the dark. Check the red nets
of pulse. You can count each bright float, tally
the catch – what bobs, what thrashes on
raging at the temple: behind the eyes, in the cave
of the ear. What a chant you are – knit through
and through with the old swells
of boatsong; haul-away, heave. And if all's well
among the strands, the hull thumps on and no wonder
our throats leap fast to shanty, all that yo-
ho following us to ground. I think we learn it skinned
into the first kind sea, scream it out when it dawns
we cease so suddenly to float. Seems we sing it one-part-
missing, every voyage after. None of this is blue, love,
not really. The clear harmony of tides, calling in
every tone in the range, whistled light-breaking wave
to abyss. There are tricks so profound, we reel
at their grace. Let us. Let us stop seeing red.

The Whoosh

UnLullaby

Do not unleash your wild words
Do not revile your weeds

Do not avoid the lightning vein
Do not unthorn the trees

Bring the feral phantoms in
Bring the Empress leech

Bring me to the drop-away
And choir me through the breach

Have mercy

Written following Hurricane Dorian, September 2019

This island opens the iris of her day, calm
curve of bay all visioning glass

deepsight clear to the seabed stones, each
a distinct sharp note, becalmed
in unstirring kelps

oh yes here
the huge animal of the world is all lull
but I turn where the trail ends in a groan
the road inhaled by her winter heaving

and on your side
of her body that same skin murmuring wet nothings
down there   where the road was
is tearing holes in itself right   this   second

and if we are any kind of people
we know what to do with an animal struggling
just to breathe

when did we close our eyes so tightly we forgot
that desperate creatures fight hard and close
more eyes as they go down
gasping

So from me running caught between breaths
to you caught in her throat
I can't say anything except   *oh god you know*
you know she never wanted this

Songbird requiem (Libera me)

(after 'Songbird' by Haroula Rose)

You spring the catch of the cage
with those thumbs, the accident

that separates us. When I fail to fly
away, the ape in you shows, her sorrowing

hoot, a sound passed pure
from your ancestors. I carry mine too,

their old blood fills the trembling cup
of my throat, spills the spool

of song I cannot stop. You have wound
the ribbons of my voice through your aloneness

for wintering months, decided it is now
the only brightness you possess.

I'd swap, I'd trade, your twilight chorus
on repeat, *just to sing, to fly away.* And I

am just a bird, my tongue near-burst
to find the notes that make you

understand, *at least*
you did not mate for life.

I would give you more than I can put in a poem

Whenever I find one, I go to your closet. Tuck it
into one of your pockets, like a lunchbox love-note. Is it more or less
than that, to give someone the slip
of a sea-day, a shiver of cloud-just-so?
Some of them fight back;
a curl of lonely moon, sharp as snipped tin: blood dots the gift,
the broken tile of a sweetgrass track that became a road buried
beneath a road beneath a road. I don't remember
when this strangeness of rain started, when the world began
to fling pieces of itself, constantly, at my feet.
I do know they wraith gone from my fingers
dare I pass them in the open. Like salt, like judgement,
like frittered days. Like secret and likely-madness, so I nest
all I can grab there in the linings of your clothes.
We never talk about the weird coin
of a shared life, all this exchanged language quite ridiculous
for filling in the blanks where my sudden, unnameable
wows and yours diverge. Aren't we all in bits, all guessing
at the picture on the box?
If I have to go, check your pockets. Mine are empty.
All the wonder I could or couldn't hold, each whoop
I couldn't quite describe – yours to find.

Day release

You say *I'm spinning again*
and I tell you the bone needle
of your spine already knows your north
from your south. To find your way home
all you need to learn is to hold the casing
still. Calm your foundations – this land
we are, it's always been
an earthquake zone. We walk
our wasted scaffolds from the hospital, stilt
to the coast, and all the seaside houses
(those ones you love most) sit on the water
fearing change. Just like you
they've made many plans to deal
with all the shaking. *What helps?* That summer
is always coming back. That the tectonics
of a rattled body stop grinding
for whole minutes under the loud beat
of the sun, that I've seen your unquiet earth
settle right down, shored up
by a hot jetty, with nothing left to do
but steam off the shutaway months. Put your chin
to the boards, shrink the world's baffle
down to woodgrain, and up close every knot
is part of the pattern – each plank
has something to show for its time spent striving
to grow. And I know you're afraid
to just rest like this, with a lifetime
of everyday shudder pinned down hard
against what's already been
undermined. And yes when the sun

goes down, the blue sea will abrupt grey
and you'll hear it, you'll hear it pick, pick at the struts
of pretty houses shivering
at early dark – and you'll be right
that the sweetest hills just fold
the dampest shade.

Turns out we're all a less desirable address
than the one advertised. But let's move in.
Let's move
      in these bodies scraped back from the edge,
let's move with intent
      to take up space.
Even the coldest light
on the darkest morning, hits the water,
                             bounces,
finds its way
to a window somewhere.

Some friends are owls

(for K)

Owl-heart, the pump flames
a night candle. Flight maps
her flicker across this landscape
of bad dreams. Rare to lift your head
of stone and find an ember
passing over, feathering
all shadow meadow. And soft
her mourning instrument comes
to ask – who, who is listening there?
A sharp moon blunts its edge to safety
on that sound.

The coast road is closed

On pinnacle hill, cliff-wind
shouts the ears pink
and who could not be a child
up here in the wild-eyed blue, tracing
farbelow bitemark-bays, the sea
mouthing forever
the beloved coast
and you knowing her curves
now like a bird, and it's loud
in your head, alone at the top
of the world, remembering
what it was to scream
taunts at the weather gods, to challenge
the sky to rain harder
      is that all you've got, is that   really   all?
to know you controlled everything just by being
alive, yeah kids believe
in themselves like that
and today this coast boasted
the biggest seas in twenty years –
roads closed, I climbed
to where cannonshot hail smashed the wild daisies
around the old gun-turret placements, crushed
petals like an offering, Sometimes
the gods just take their time
to answer you back

Recovery

They're skeletons, you said, *but on the outside.*
Metal bucket half-filled with bodies, dull bell sounding each

harvest. Theirs. Ours. Hey, miracle
knot of muscle, content in the casket, the dark, I'd ask you

how the hell to live
like that, but you're already eaten. To my shame, drowned

in butter and salt, pretty scraps sucked clean. I, too,
have been building a cage

of bone, shrugging it scary obvious. Trowelling hard
from soft – the less heart

we take in, the more pulse, frantic at the joint. This broken
desire, to crack the hinges

of the chest, empty it of treasure, un-mussel, snap hollow, castanet
the boy down to nothing but brittle music – the way cartoon crabs

brandish a bivalve
for rhythm. Who will hold me aloft and listen. What is emerging

to dance could grow claws of its own, if you did.
Listen now: I could blame them

for acting without me – they'd hook morsel
after desperate morsel, scrape hard at the bucket, find themselves

completely
unable to let go.

Reclaiming the birdboy

I run again past that familiar sadness
of rusting struts – old plane
drowned in the harbour

and I thank you, sinews, for holding up
despite my knowing
a body may become a flock of bones
never hollow enough to fill with flight

I tried to kill the bird
many times, by emptying it fast or slow
and how right these hovering gulls fighting
over fish and chip paper from the takeaway
that stank the terror of oil

and I never thought these land-legs
would muscle strong, nor these scarred
unfeathered arms
would fleet the wind like this – in updrafts

an unclouded message:
feel your shape made to float free
you perfect engine
from all the mud
that ever denied you air

Defibrillated

She was waiting – just
    like I planned it, years
on the brink

My bare toes plug into the sand
    –hold–
I am thrumming, how
the tide hisses about resolve

When the foam steams in
    I am unearthed, loss-
laxed sinews livewires
    broken switches arcing

She slams home the current
    –connected–
the world jolts, deep
    secrets bang from my splits
shocking, how familiar
    her fear of slow evaporation

I reel home on blistered soles
to lie about no plans and wet clothes

Your mouth twists wavelets
the room darkens, the lights
    of the burned-out city
that has become my body
    flicker on one by one by one
a gull of sound leaves you

With that, my long drying-up is ended –
the electric sea
floods from me
in torrents   in torrents   in torrents

Solastalgia

Half-done sun flares the water, light lancing clear depths
beneath an ape who swims these days for the joy of it
and a body's old map uncreases, reading happy accidents aloud

Tuck proud thumbs, and hands recall easy the flipper in the bone
and that they ruddered for a living, five million years gone

And below, a starling rush of rays murmurs round a mountain
too sudden for their species' long atlas, quaked up overnight,
five thousand years gone

And above, a shoal of swifts, arrows shot true
from their strings, zip the ghost-tree targets
of their hatching grove, felled overnight, five years gone

And that half-done sun is warm on anything like shoulders
for another 5 billion strokes or so, and the wind picks up cool now
and the clouds flickerframe —play at peaks
and valleys, beasts and branches—
then wisp gone.

And who doesn't love a blank,
blue
sky

Grit / love

Some days I'm salt flats
cracking with wist
for that time before hard sun
pressed me to heavy crust

back when I was sea-wind
tangling you up with myself
I knew that was love, and I ask you
do you miss the waves

and your hand replies easy air-shapes
and there my rime glitters
tendering your fingertips – you crumble me
to tiny jewels, already falling

see how beautiful
even grit
and oh that old crush, nothing really escapes it

Take two (2) in the morning, after disclosing as needed : ii

Weak morning startles in, an accusation: hoar
frost, so cold after its homonym broke your nightbefore mouth
and that was the first time it marked someone I knew. He'd pinned it
right where you'd remember, a label inside you/r school clothes
waiting
like it was your new name.

All night you'd snotted out rage and I fed it
on the ugly bones of your house, outside
the world changed, fronded out this frosted shell and
hid its guts, just waiting
for us to flee from all that can't-unsay, feet
punch-punching through ice crust skin like all the eggs you'd walked
on and I swore
I swear, those crushed green atolls strung out wet with life
behind you
glowed
invitation. Nothing for it but to lie
down, confirm our vital shapes, press hands
faces tongues to conquer the scabbing creep
of white, white.

She revived fierce and ready
mutual mouth-to-
mouth shock shuddering her up through the ground
and Kuramarotini
Ur-roared your frozen ear awake with kindred recognition.
I heard her tell you, *girl, you get up now, you stride*

across what's exposed, over
my chain of mountain tips.
You feel a small island, but you and her, you're the jutpeaks of secret
continents, deep-hid shapes your own unknown, and
no hard seas can drown you.

Gravity music with shellfish

The skyhook beak has opened, your body
a flipped coin, whistle-rush wind sings your edge
wild flight, oh brief, oh surely here comes the whole
new life in some strange air's ocean for this knot
of wet-fragile trapped inside this shell that crept dark
for years, made music
only the once, it's not the albatross that sinks you, just
the lust of heavy water for the earth and don't we all
become a sound of desperate sweetness right
before we split

Abandoned tunnel dare – All Hallows Eve

At the dare's threshold, our feet hook the earth – refuse
to move. I forget light. Climbing here, bonfires dimmed
to fireflies – the erratic runway of the beach
swims giddy-far below, and friendly flame
has long since left my bones. No triumph dance
for us now – all bucking urge plucked out
by what is real. Wet fern fingers drip
chill chamber-music
to change an ear's shape forever.

Afterwards, we will always hear the waxing dark.

What sort of person decided fear
is a game, a human challenge to the longest night –
none are warriors here, the old black story-heart
of this place knows us
as a lit candle knows its moths.
The young fly blind – with their masks and their mumming
and their tender, thrill-shrilling hearts – ah, gifts.

Offer your walking-in as a sacrifice. Litany yourself, repeat:
may the crunch of footed things be leaves, be gravel
may that tang on my panting tongue be watered rust
may the sunrise find us bigger than we began –
the only sugar we will beg from here
the sweet stun of light, more and more
minutes palmed into our lucky, lengthening days.

The last string

That little town where every kid
starts out with a festival of balloons

each step they're followed by every colour
before they know the names of any of them

to grow up means to let go of strings
and one by one, they do

when did you realise your body
was a thin shape you were stuck inside

when did you let go of the knowing
that one day you'd be a dolphin

or a butterfly, for-certain-for-real
and your promising skin would stretch

so bright and right, to float you free
when did the second-to-last colour

become just a shadow on the sun
and did you wave it gone

like the proud new adults in that town
left holding just the one

Living still

Columbine, that wild showoff,
rattles her best bonnets, face full-tipped
to the wind's bright tease. Quiver after quiver,
each seed in the heart's chamber, shaking the bloom.
What else do we mean by 'alive' – barely contained,
something always moving. The river shows her hands
braiding water, warm-over-cool, dark-over-blue.
Clouds fold a busy origami of light. Insects dart the rope,
the crease. Everything on its own time. The giddy earth.
This loudness sounding in your chest.

A foal takes shelter wherever it stands

At the end of the street, that field
eye-high with weeds – a sanctuary

for lost horses. Sad horses were snapped crayons
to country kids, but the bones

of the old villa, also haunting that field – pure myth.
In one room, ectoplasm: the huge pale ghost

of a moulded plaster ceiling, turned to dust. You spoke
to me only because I always had some limb

or another in a cast, which meant gruesome
and intriguing, so I was not unlike the lure

of a derelict house, and the plaster cast I fashioned
from ghosts and rainwater for you was heavy

and convincing. In a thing abandoned, the weight
of the fear it will happen again lives deep

in the struts. You coveted what was broken
more than once, and I pretended your Dad

was mine, even when he was shouting
about your arm. It was one of many bargains

we didn't voice, a couple of mouths busy grazing, beasts
unshod and unclaimed. I heard you never escaped

that town, and never broke a thing.
I never went back, and I don't know

what would be worse – a new house
sitting whole on a grave

or a completely empty field
with not a horse in sight.

Circinate vernation

Here the lushly hurting green
spring spirals hard on hips of dripping hills
wild-unsmoothed by conquerors, old
ferns tendered
back to cradle-coil

Sap corkscrews vines of not-grown
kids, and even the sodden lambs
are unhinged, fast-growing two new canny teeth
to escape the mortal chute

My own fat fingers greasen-soft
from fenceplucked yanks of fleece, rippled white
the curls bleat also down my neck
my neck so unaware of the wire

Pull-snared by colder seasons
tighten the winding-down, that white
wool my age
of hard awareness my shakehands
unsoftened by kind lanolins

Pen, pour out, flood now torrid spring
pin fast that greenwing vital boy, for
swift the bone-chariot ices
my road into the drowsing dark
and all lambfleece goes
to fronds, the curling smokeblack plumes
for all four nodding horses

Inspired by the sensation Dylan Thomas metres out inside an atypical brain, and more literally by a combination of 'Fern Hill' 'Do not go gentle into that good night' and 'Death Shall Have no Dominion'

The giant fish takes back the myth

The morning before she was to become a story
the sea was baited quiet, the kind that silks

all desire down to swish. To decide to leap
from one cool world to another just for breakfast

is to bare your colours to the scaling knife of the wind,
and she did – her fireback beacon launched

for the brief protein of flying legs. How often we fail
to see that dark hull waiting; we beasts so full up

with the rush of living for our risks.
And the shape of the poised hero held no meaning, to a fish

but oh the shimmerhook, like all the moons
her eye's nightcoin had ever purchased

from deep beneath the water, and there is the lust, the swish-
and-want. The glowworm crescent to silver her belly.

We all want to shine in fullness.
Only heroes are given names in these stories.

For her need she was translated
into an island, and I am running the delicate gasp of her jaws

in the shape of this coast, forever straining for the hook
and still called only *fish*

even with all we have made of her. Every time I desire
to transcend my quiet water, I forget the heroes

and leap from her skin, and hope
that landing empty

but with one eye fixed on the moon
every night after this will be enough.

Companion planting

I come back to what I first learned about ending
and there's the nipped grace of your hands — secateurs

beaking spent calendula. After each clip, a tremor
took you, and the sun on the blades quivered

a genuflection for the beheaded. Bless us, too,
and what finishes flowering in our summer flesh

before we're ready for the harvest.
You crossed, yourself, without ceremony

and I like to think they planted you in that apron,
pockets spilling dried seedheads, rattling

begin begin begin. Louder for their name containing *end*.
I like to think that wherever you went next

you made a bright green entrance, wearing cotyledons
like a new skin, two baby leaves squalling from every pore.

In that vision, you're still saying *that cinnamon scent
they exhale, it wards off pests*. Even the sap-sucking beast

we never see until it's plagued its way
through the roots of the whole patch, so when the wind

last swivelled sick south, hot copper dust wafted
something holy through these quieted, quivering streets

and I knew you were shaking your head. *Not the end.*
Begin begin begin. Every cradled possible

a kind of cure, tendering the birth of many suns
from the curved shadow of a seed.

The Drift

New cloth

Your pattern pinned itself to the fray of me
the first day. Not yet stitched, aligning
fragile tissue, judging bias – the wounded
cut carefully
always holding their breath.

When they remade you, I slept
on a hospital couch with your dress, bundled
like a woollen heart, to my nose. Five hours
inhaling-exhaling bargains
a short time to outfit a whole woman
into her own dear self.

We tied knots with every colour we could find.

Understand, love always gets down to the wisp
beyond fabric, to stroke
the finest thread of a person – our making looms
us legacies of holes –
you fear cutting yourself short, me
born running with scissors, and all of us
rippling fast towards the great unravelling

Yet the thump-thumping treadle of the heart can still say
now you're mending – billow with the wind.

Perfect circle

Begin again—born to cold-swaddle-
sea and she wraps me to nurse

this grievance with gravity.
The sinews of snap-and-blast

let go. Grit floats from my hinges.
It is very early, the water's skin

thinned to eyelid, and whole worlds cradle
rocking behind the fold. I 'gator, sightline only

for the ripple, smalled disrupt
of my body mapped

onto hers. All the disquiet
I am, she writes larger, out and out

forever but gentle as a pulse
of jellyfish and yes out here

I understand the thumb
on every scale heavy

more than anywhere else.
Rain begins. She embraces each child

as he falls, soon overcome
by a chatter of circles, spreading

brief astonishment— O, O, O—
then, again, murmured part of her vast. Me

too, me, too. No way to tell
why my face is wet.

Gardening with B. F. Skinner and St. Bede

To look at a human face and perceive a black box
is a philosopher's way of saying 'what flies through the lighted room
between your ears is unknowable to me'. But there I go already
mixing my philosophers and my monks. The point of the black box
is that it is lightless from the outside looking in,
and I can't ever imagine
being so closed down that no face held a candle up to the eyes – no
lambent glow left flickering in the window
to guide the traveller home, to indicate a hearth to share.
So I'm still thinking about all of you as rooms,
and inside the conservatory that I am, there are petals
all over the floor. A bird rushed through the hydrangeas
I keep in here just yesterday, and now all the soft colours we wrap
our children tightly with, those same ones that label
the boxes before we can philosophise or parable at all,
are drifting deep. And maybe my subconscious chose those flowers
for this room because they're a litmus.
Don't you want to see what's going on
underneath in the dark, where all the growing really happens –
who's hurting acid, who's blanding base. Can't you see
that the light beacons in and out
through bird-shaped holes in the walls, and if you look
at a person without thinking about boxes
sometimes you find a garden
telling you what it needs the most.

Franz Josef Glacier 2020 (will they say)

In the pitching dark, the origin sea
      is flooding – a black vein swelling deep below
a white-chased wound. The ice
      does not yet speak of the secret bleed
but keeps all her movement spare and slow. It befits a victim
      blued tongue cracking effort and berg, to accept
that each hundred years slicks down its own groan
      but these short months are a spreading bruise, frozen flesh
fevering hit after hit to wear
      a giant down. And when they examine what's left
before it liquids the records into pressed ocean
      will they say: here is a streak of whole continent
gone to dust, slapping down palms orange with ash, paint
      of fur and tooth and bone. A smear there, the fatty soot
we ourselves thumb into
      when a mountain stokes the forge it always was. Will they say
why so clean from this point on, what stopped
      all the engines here – oh just let it melt. Even glaciers
want to forget this next one. Return the witnessing to water
      where nothing has even begun to remember.

Matariki (southern right)

She returns here, every year to the day
a nomad continent
tugged in by the bright hooks of Pleaides.
Each nonchalant breach is a game –
call-and-response of old shape
echoing shape – her spine speaks the hills
cradling the city, and her fathoming
eye settles in with the stars
to reclaim the harbour. We named her
for her compass-worlds – *gods' gaze*

Seen by the divine, we seek more
drama in our water, the brash barge bobs
ringed about with fireworks, and the airwaves
skitter jokes – how we delay ourselves for this guest –
what insult
to her chambering boom, what rudeness
to the waiting gasp of the night sky
spraying wildflower sparks since this dirt slept, why
are things we have not wrought
never enough for us

And what is all our noisy celebration
to a whale, but desperation –
the whole ocean a constant *we are here* – floating
cities, sliding sheet-ice, from the Antarctic
she brings her calf, seeking
the old quiet bowl of water. They have followed

populations of rays, rippling rings, murmurations – that word
it sounds like human speech, but here
means deep silence, and a multitude
flowing as one living thing

Earthquake weather

Three faultlines knap what's buried
into blades, scraping deep inside
the animal. On this south stretch
of her hide we hatch playing

a game – *did you feel that? Wind,*
or quake? Pick your unsettle – the rage
of a toddler-storm smacking over the blocks
of the house, or Rūaumoko sharpening

the range, whetting dark to draw
a jaggy line beneath your feet. No wonder
all the myths with jawbones, we clench
until it aches in the weather-

smile, grimace local as the civil
defence drills, both socketed in
before our adult teeth. Say *severe,*
say *weather warning,* say *120km gusts,*

we say *yep just another Tuesday*
and traction for a coast long since skinned
all backbone. You can't lie to a scale – by nature
we're exposed, our struts, too, plained

to wreck by the most truthful half
of the year. The knife hurts, it hurts but swallow
this: how lucky to winter in the teeth. Be hard-
bitten, or go – break up

with the scour, pretend you're civil, slink
your season's story north to soft-
tongued hills and shut-in-lazy-vowels, rolled
sleeping dull beneath white quilts, send yourself

that Christmas card, kid, weird with glitter.
But know well-whistled bone will always play
the haunt – some places are not meant to rest.
One kind far windless morning, you'll lean on in

to the shoulder of a southerly-gone, fall
flat, await the bite, the thrill of clouds belly-ripped
by canine rocks tusking the greyspittle lip
of the sea. Your smile then, too, honed by island blast

to predator-and-nerve. In snow-mute our kind dream
no angels, but in naked angles, no festive costume
of fir-sway for your party's ridge, her hackles
the tangled wire of trees, prone

to grow sideways, rooted just enough in a scrape
of dirt. What are you, what are you
celebrating? Where's the rasp
of June to say *winter wraps no gifts* but the wild

gamble of your reckless creature
still clinging, come spring. No miracle – you are
a snarl. A snarl unshaken, unshaken somehow still
from the seethe of the earth.

Matariki (the winter-maid)

We climb until we hear her. Wailing windfloats the hilltop – finding
        four cold bright ears, tipped keen
                to the winter-maid's starsong grief. Like the harbour

fireworks, some hearts are a conflagration always
        ready to set off, tonight Rā shimmies
                the black ice, away to the shining arms of another

and Hine-Takurua forgives – only her strong south currents
        wax a little saltier each year, and there
                in the long chill shadows of touchpaper gods, I palm

you the foil-skinned planet
        plucked from the coals of the bonfire, left tide-
                eaten far below

Split deep softsun orange, the sweet kūmara steams, burns fingers
        and eager mouths – a minute more tasted light, and full bellies
                glow against the dark

Shellfish lovers

Morning splits   a faint pink line, gulls horning
          the sky's mouth wider

you still sandflea, curled greedy around sleep
          hoarding empty shells, bonfired, and me still full

of yesterday. Old devourings forgotten, my hands rough-memory
for new shucked jewels – yours atop mine with their knack
          stab – twist – crack

A careful blade gentles in before you know you're harvested. I have
woken
          glistening jelly, fresh-seen –
open   to the cool brine of a new day

How to return, in the end

Leave a place whole.
Return missing what's missing –
you, and the riverbank,
both bitten into.

My feet often make decisions alone – I run
off the trail, where a kid once disappeared. He persists
in each fern-crack footfall – maybe
fishing, or in hot study of mud and insect, then
the noisy space of an absence.

They raked the current that spring, buzzed by arrowing swifts
returned, hunting for their birthing-trees – lost
to the housing development. Even birds
can't nest with ghosts.

I don't know if they found a body, but this body knows
it's not right to trap a swelling river
within a thin skin – the water of a person
flows back to its source, so here
we are, shoes lost, toes mudded,
seeing swallows.

The sign warns
of runoff, but I'm floating with bones
that remember things clean.

Gorky Park, 1999

The ferris wheel spoke in rust
and flakes of twilight. Snared by the hooks
of our own hackles, we turned and turned,
giddied by the dangerous and squeaky wheel
of the wrong hemisphere. The envelope that held
our reserves was long torn at the corner and that moon,
that ripped Russian moon, spilled its dust. It settled everywhere
and changed nothing. There's a point at which you're so far away
from home you may as well be walking the beams
in space, and when the strut broke we were astronauts
just for a second, weightless. You, my shooting star,
trailing glitter and the tether that never truly tied you
to anything at all, snapped at long last. When our bodies
left the ride, what had trembled inside them
remained in orbit. Don't be afraid. It was nothing
anyone needed to keep safe.

First gather your ingredients

A lattice of early light. Butter soft. You'd approve
that today is barely awake and already busy
baking – a dawn insistent
on offering us something well-mixed. Sweet, yes,
but still raw. This is the part, I think, where we're allowed
to lick the bowl clean and never be full.
Your hand in mine is a twitchy animal
from another world, all its hollow armour worn now
on the outside. The baker drizzles her spoon
across the bed, basting well, and inside its shell some scanty meat
is juiced through and through with sunlight – in the world
I am imagining they loll out tongues and gulp it down greedy
like plants. In the world I am imagining, every day the sun rises
is a feast. I fit the whorled planet of my thumb's tip
into the snuffbox at your wrist, stir up the motes
that have gathered there, excited to be free
of the flesh. Your pulse shivers
through your leaves, causes murmuring
in the populace. Until now it's been as reliable
as celsius, each stir of the batter meaning
be patient, love, for the cake. Oh how you celebrated
everything I was, now it's my turn – me, on this day,
this day so eager to begin she forgot her apron
and doesn't care one whit for the mess. The blinds open,
you're alight, sparks unsnuffed and streaming
to find the window and I'm not sure
if the sound that fills the room means I'm singing
or making my wish.

Fossil sea-snail

From the world's frozen lid
carefully cored, your final opening opens
our eyes to the Permian. The Great Dying was done
when you crept, 3-chambered heart bouncing
the shape of your life into nacre
and your breaking releases otherworlds, petrified seas
cresting chalk-white horses, your shattering split a skyberg
needling peacock auroras
inside, you are a lost polar dance
may what comes after crack our bones like this
and see the light inside our starry steps, our short spiral
snailed, sunken, broken open
to all new radiance.

Bringing back the lost

Seashells grit their last, beneath
the new trident of my toes
A stranger wake, these marks I leave on the day
        are pointed – a trail
of arrows, heavied into the sand
   – here is the way back from your extinction –

I run the spine of midden-hill, knowing full well
it is his body
   – see the fallowed sea-monster –
Eyes open, muscle a litany, enough
to tattoo that sleeping skin
with each   willing   foot   fall
   – wake, wake now, we need your taniwha tricks –

Heavy each step to groan breath
from the ground
by downhill my feet are fast-
panting dunes to lifespeed
   – he stretches and laughs
me into old shapes –

The man walking his leashed dog will dream tonight
   – eyes tight closed –
rattled by the invisible
brush with abacus feathers, hissing
throat-hum of bird stink, shuddering
tender ferns

151

The dog will dream precisely what he saw –
hook-shadow huge
moa unlost, beautiful belief-
haunches powering
the runner, who opened his eyes twice
and let the past come for him

Welcome to The Garden

The child found the archway
and entered the garden. Wet hands
pressed brief starfish into the moss
cushioning the bricks as she steadied herself, all new
to this walking thing. After her, a green landscape wept
thick rain, puddled a creation myth of tardigrades
singing for the five tributaries, the goddess
who had seen fit to seed them from her baby fingers.
You would have said the child carried nothing
and the cloud-cataracts of her eyes did not reflect
any sky you would recognise. By the third step
she had doomed a race of grass-dwelling moons,
had startled a new shade of pink to mean *eve-*
ning is inevitable but also *morning will be beautiful*
and she could replicate the roly-polys
of worms being silently valuable, eating and excreting
all the riches of her lengthening shadow.
There were nine strong stakes planted firmly
in the weeds, each hoping out a different kind of leaf
that would feed her and hurt her by turns.
There was no wrong choice. Nothing was burning.
Her grip was very strong now
and the pluck was sure
and clean, though the earth sighed from the hole
in her side as the thorn eased free. Worms rolled in
quietly to fill up the wound. When the child left, the garden
was more alive or more dead everywhere
she'd ever touched. She carried tenderly her poison
and her panacea, and the dark mouth of the arch called
—you did everything right. Now you must return—
and that held no fear for her at all.

Hand over hand

In celebration and memory of Dai Fry

We were sleeping, here in the underbelly,
when you picked up the oar to row. Rivers

of waxing light bob their boats of dust into day
and I'm thinking about hands and how, offered, they open

into stars, stylised suns, an eye – shocked
to be so seen, like a child

might crayon. I'm thinking about them as anything
but quiet gloves. I'm thinking about how often

mine leap to help me say *all this *this** and how
you knew that meant everything lurking

behind the breakers is too big to fathom
without some shell getting swept up. I'm thinking

about hauling on the rope, how delicate the callous
against the wheel, about five fragments of enormous

in the northern sky, how last night you'd have seen
Cassopeia offering her hand, wet with silver.

Palm up, fingers open to catch what drifts
into the dark – flashed to brilliance

and afterimage. Your wave, frozen in time.

Bittern score

No   sense

of time's beat   passing   each note

the dip of an evening   baton

symphony   for pump   uncoupled   unbirds

we're too busy   anticipating   what's coming

unstuck   to hear the music

from the pipe   *like a liquid boom*   and I see you unshaped

like a liquid   *– boom–*   yes, fountain

one foot

in the mud and a body flung to droplets   one bar breaking

gravity   then heavy

raining *please*

That which can be made visible

Sun's first sleep-breath
sweets the dropped shoulder

of Te Puia o Whakaari, her bones
in early mistlight all grace

and delicate pickings, gulled
clavicles of a hard dancer, stilled.

Coiled tension is resting. It is hard
to recognise a haunting

in the rose-gilt of a sunrise. Do you know
her name? When you recognised it,

did you forget to exhale? Release
your living now to cloud

the pane we do not see – deep
scratches creep across this vision.

The guardians are always here to remind you –
this light, it may change any moment.

In memory of those lost in the eruption of Whakaari on 9 December 2019. One translation of the te reo Māori name of this volcano forms the title of this poem.

A shell returns to the sea

This room an air bubble
in a concrete slab corridor
and you fish-gasping nightmares
I'll never see the sea again

I tell you it's all around you
I tell you all this
cement is just sand and water

I tell you even the hospital windows, gritted
shut against this ugliness
were born on a beach

I dig so deep my words fill the room
with water, the wild chop
of your chest
calms to swells, and sleep

driftwoods you gone, bones floating hollow
as my hand curled around the whelk of your ear
willing traffic noise
to sound an ocean

The point is magic

On the gardener's hand a beetle has arrived. Strut legs
cushion the touchdown – a tiny Mars rover. There is a puff
of skin flakes, a fine drift of compost, an unheard cheer
of victory. The visitor is beautifully shielded
against the conditions on this planet, her cladding shiny
as tinfoil, but vibrant green – emerald so astonishing
the row of new seedlings far below the horizon clamour
jealously in their earth bed. The woman who has become
all new terrain raises it to eye height, the hand
and the ship of the beetle, and when the familiar tremor
grips her, she pauses. An astronomical body
becomes vastly patient, even with her own treacherous weather.
The magical vessel (the beetle, although you could be forgiven
at this point for thinking this referred also to the gardener)
does not react. Custom-designed hooks have already grappled
into the great fissures of brown rock and it is as steady,
in the earthquakes it was trained to expect, as in any solar wind
in space. She breaths aeons of gas on the carapace
and somewhere a creation myth is written.
There are minutes so taut with an ordinary act-
become-suddenly-significant that time hiccups a bubble
into the glass, suspends it forever. This was one. At some point
the ship left and the planet realigned herself
with the earth, at some point the sun wavered great shadows
through the garden, at some point the seedlings
sprouted and gave their own young
to those solar winds, and at some point
all trembling stilled, and the map, in relief, was finally complete
for the next surveyors. What was the point, the point was
it happened. The point was the spell, not the ingredients.

The point is ridiculously
small, the point at which two insignificant universes
collide. They do it over and over again, until the point where
something changes forever. Where everything
turns out just the same.

Pōhutukawa

(Aotearoa's 'Christmas tree')

On the downslope from the solstice
our true December trees

are brazen, bloody-bright. You can keep
your dark, doomed pines, all smooth tradition

for the baubles – sadness-
-in-waiting beneath fake snow –

that never worked out here
on the edge. Our festive day is gaudy

with the tinsel-glare of sun, we grew up ripe
to glut ourselves on light this time

of year. The young, the old, they really crave
the exact same simple gift. And pōhutukawa,

she shows you every year how to age
shamelessly. Carried on her auntie's back

toward the squalling new year, you'll hear
her last dirty old laugh with your eyes

open (none of your damn grace required), flinging
all that made the new gods whisper *scarlet wanton*

to the hot south wind, spreading fierce
naked claim and delight. Every path,

every last road out of here, it pants
with spent red. It's so easy

to get weighed down trying to make light
for the whole family. Oh, it's not what you give.

It's what you leave,

it's how.

Fountain / pump

I filled your ear with the fountain
playing with the bay, coin-slot joy
you loved to feed

At that moment you stopped
making more of yourself
sea　　　　　*becomes flight*　　　*becomes cloud*

I sat with you, pumping sympathy
machinery stilled

bright silver
gone to wisps

Personal acknowledgements

Without the encouragement, wisdom, and mentorship of Matthew M.C. Smith, EIC of *Black Bough Poetry*, this book wouldn't exist. Thank you for seeing something in me I'd long lost sight of in myself.

Without the unconditional love and unwavering support of my beautiful Cate, I wouldn't be around to have written it. The wonder that is this woman billows in the wind and water of these poems for all time, and there's not enough thanks in this whole world to give her. The latter is also true of my mother, Diana, who never stopped believing in me no matter how dark things became, and of my 'chosen family' – too many to name, but especially Susan A (Eggie), Arrin & Kate, Vic & Jono, the Harpers, Helen, Lisa, Laura, Paul Q, and Glenn & Tina. For your love and belief in me across many struggling-years far gone and recent, the best thanks I can give you is in these pages.

My endless, humble gratitude and respect to the tangata whenua of Aotearoa – only by the generosity of your tupuna, as tangata tiriti was I permitted to enter into this world here; to grow up as your guest, walking your land as it breathes. To the mighty Whanganui and those in my early life who held me in the flow of her stories, language, and myths in ways that deeply shaped a spirit cut off from his own line, my deepest debt. This book would not be this book were I made anywhere else, and never will I take that debt to people or place for granted – whatungarongaro te tangata toitū te whenua.

To environmental philosopher Glenn Albrecht for first coining the word 'Solastalgia', that perfect summation of the ache accompanying environmental loss.

To those from Ward 27 and other gaps – the Jonis, Simons and Jesuses in all their forms, my love. Know there are people who will always see you true, even when you can't. To Dr Perry, for sparing a damaged kid so much worse. To the survivors, always. Never stop speaking, every and any which way you can. To you rainbow kids, may you feel your worth early and know it always. To Brenda, Shane, Jay, and all those souls who felt there was no choice left but to leave this weeping place. I'll never forget you. You, too, live in these words.

To primo grue-conjurer Anna, for translating a giddy dream of cover art into a solid being via her beautiful brain and hands. You turned a wild vision into a painting that (impossibly) sings every nuance of every poem in this collection, and I'm so immensely grateful for the depth of your seeing.

To many dear poet-friends: Kyla for her open heart and constant support-hoots, Moira & Robert, for seeing me clearly through the cracks, and all my colleagues at *Barren*, particularly Maddie & Lee, for their utter care. To Gaynor for reminding the goat of his rainbows, Geraldine for apples and joy-prayers, Anja for manatee-dances and dog-noses, Kate mother-of-sweetpeas for her patience, Esther for realness and care-packages, Deborah and Sam for endless drops of bright water, Sage for bringing her brave green heart.

To those friends not mentioned elsewhere here who have lifted my work and my spirits time and again out of simple goodness: Peach, Rachel, Polly, Ness, Lynn, Anindita, Todd, Vic, Velid, Tara, Kiley, Julia, Judith, Ed, Patrick, Melissa, Tigs, Sarah, Jay, Jude, Jo, Becs, Ruth, Susan, Lynne, Mat, Bren, Jenny, Preston, Mark, Pax, Megha, Joe, Jakky, Dua, Paula, Vismai, Gretchen, Leela, Andy, Robin, Gayle, Joyce, Danielle, Jesse, Gabe, Blue, Lynda, Sarah-Jane, Praise, David, Martins, Eileen, Serge, Dominic, Alessa, Devon, Miszka, Jane, Alice, Mo, Jess, Steph, Ranjabali, Lindz, Karlo, Laurie, Laura, Zaina,

Stephen, Michael, Sian, Alison, Kaye, Maggs, Carol, Katy, Ronnie, Shelle, Soraya, Ann, Karen, Lucy, Beth, Matt, Erin, Pax, Sue, Iris, Tricia, Georgia, Eilín, Dave, Cat, Kaye, Megha, Trivarna, Fidel, Brian, Lisa, Ryan, Tracey, Larissa, Elizabeth, Richard, M., Priyanka, Satya, Helen, Voima, Daisy, Clay, Ian, Roger, Aud, Chris, Cyndie, Ben, Taylor, Isaura, Yvonne, Annie, Ruairí, Shareen, Heather, Penny, Cassie, Russ, Sascha, Anne, Pat, Lisa, Nadia, Steve, Stuart, Eliot, Raye, Merril, Ellie, Matt, Suzi, Margaret, John, Mary, Hannah, Han, & Jason. And to the huge light that is the loyal, magical selkie-soul Rhona, and her fae Mum, Patricia – you are forever-family to me. Everyone on this list has kept me going in ways that reach and hold well beyond the scope of poetry.

To David L of *Red Ink*, and David O of *Fevers of the Mind*, for making the first poet-interviews of my nervous life so wonderful (and David O for everything he does for poetry). Huge thanks also to the big, bright heart-projects keeping poetry so alive and shouting; *Cheltenham Poetry Festival* – Anna S, Howard, Zoe, Annie, Josephine & the whole crew of that ship of wonderful poets who have given me their space, time, and joy, Mark's love-labour *Iamb*, gorgeous Damien & his *Eat the Storms* Podcast, *The Poetry Archive* for giving 'New Cloth' a place to be found by those who needed it, and to the whole *Black Bough* #TopTweetTuesday family of poets for their weekly positivity-chorus, cheered on by Matt Smith.

Gratitude always to Paul B, poet, friend, and editor of *Wombwell Rainbow*, and artists Jane Cornwell, Mary Frances, Kerfe Roig, John Law, Sue Harpham, and James Knight, who provided deep and inspirational images for Paul's ekphrastic challenge months – birthdays for early drafts of many, many poems in these pages.

To each editor and reader who ever gave my work a place to speak, my full heart.

To my wonderfully kind advance readers and also dear friends; Anna, Alan, Damien, Geraldine, Jack, Kari, Lee, Matt, and Paul, whose ready and effusive generosity made me cry for days and feel like this book was everything I hoped it might be.

To Adele & Betty for beach-hugs. To Dai, in deepest peace-seas. And very special paper-boat thanks to my earliest online poetry fan, Tina (Kina).
If I've failed to list your name, I hope you still know the gifts you gave me. There are so many of you, and not nearly enough pages.

My penultimate thanks are for the heart-coven of Femme Salvé – to dear, dear Amanda, Eli, and Beth. You so unexpectedly threw this manuscript a life-ring when it was all but swallowed by water grown suddenly choppy and cold, and well – you saved the poet, too. My gratitude is its own whole animal, swimming for his life.

My last thanks is for you. Yes, you – with that miracle brain translating all these words into something personal. What you're holding in your hands is a life, and it continues to breathe outside this engine's mechanism by the strangest and most unexpectedly beautiful magic I can imagine – time given freely by every human who ever read a word I wrote.

Publication acknowledgements for included poems

My heartfelt thanks to the editors of the following literary magazines, journals, presses, reviews, projects, blogs, and archives, who have published or reprinted some of the works in these pages in their previous or current forms. My extra-humble thanks also to many of these editors for Pushcart Prize and Best of the Net nominations for several poems included here, and for selecting some of the pieces in this book as competition winners, short-listers, or long-listers. Your faith in my work is beautiful, and my gratitude for that is enduring.

Moonchild Magazine, Trampset, Feral: A Journal of Poetry and Art, The Failure Baler, Black Bough Poetry, The Wombwell Rainbow, Hobart After Dark, Feed, Perhappened, Fly on the Wall Press, Honey & Lime (Oceans & Time), Moist Poetry Journal, Fevers of the Mind Poetry & Art, Rhythm & Bones Press, Headline Poetry & Press, Burning House Press, IceFloe Press, PoetRhy Garden Project, Neologism Poetry Journal, Auckland University Press (forthcoming), VSS365 Anthology (Mark A. King), The Bangor Literary Journal, Elephants Never, Anti-Heroin Chic, Claw & Blossom, Coffin Bell, The Hellebore Press, Kissing Dynamite, Re-Side Magazine, Cease, Cows, Mineral Lit Mag, Truly U Review, The Poetry Archive, Iamb, Wildfire Words e-zine (Frosted Fire Press/Cheltenham Poetry Festival), The Broken Spine Arts Collective, Sarah Connor's Advent Calendar, Red Ink (David Raphael Lewis interview series), Hedgehog Poetry Press.

Aotearoa glossary / notes on the poems

Travelling light
Te Rerenga Wairua: a place at the northernmost tip of Aotearoa. Its name means *the leaping-off place of spirits*.

Microcosm
Hine-nui-te-pō: literally *the big woman of the night*. In Māori mythology she is the spirit of the night, and/or the spirit of death.

Taniwha country
Taniwha: a sea-monster/sea-serpent. The peninsula this poem walks is the fallen body of a great taniwha named Whātaitai. In the spectacular story of the creation of Te Whanganui-a-Tara (*the great harbor of Tara*, aka Wellington, the capital city of Aotearoa New Zealand) his taniwha companion, Ngake, swims still in the waters of Te Moana o Raukawa (aka Cook Strait) between the two main islands.

Pariwhero (Red Rocks)
Pariwhero: An isolated coastal trail in Te Whanganui-a-Tara, with ancient volcanic rock formations of a distinctive, unusual red. There are many stories about their colour; some about Kupe, the Polynesian explorer who first discovered Aotearoa, and some about Māui, the legendary figure who, in Aotearoa's creation myth, fished up the North Island. Every story involves blood.

Last chance to settle
Aotearoa was one of the earliest 'significant landmasses' to become isolated, breaking from Gondwanaland 85 million years ago. It's also one of the last to see human inhabitants; the first Polynesian explorers estimated to have arrived only in the 13th century. *Tapu* means sacred/protected/under the protection of spirits. All human

remains are tapu. Those in this poem are the earliest evidence of a Polynesian settlement in Aotearoa, found at Wairau Bar.

Wellington airport is built on reclaimed land

The international airport at Huetepara (Lyall Bay) in Te Whanganui-a-Tara (Wellington) opened as a grass runway in the 1930s, then closed in the 1940s for major earthworks and re-development to extend it. The author's mother clearly remembers extensive sand dunes before they disappeared as land was claimed for the tarmac. The title also refers to the fact that this land was originally taken from Māori by white colonisers, and to the use of soil shifted from the seabed and other areas, changing the waterline on both sides of the peninsula.

Ice

The area this poem walks is Taputeranga (Island Bay) in Te Whanganui-a-Tara. There is evidence of Māori pā (settlements/hillforts) in the hills and on the island. Today the steep, hilly roads round the coast are painted with blue safety zones denoting high ground for tsunami. *Pūrerehua* are traditional Māori musical instruments (aka bull-roarers) made of wood, stone or bone whirled on a string to create an eerie sound associated with calling in rain, and with funerals. This word also means butterfly or moth.

Sea-gods self-soothe

Tangaroa: in Māori creation myth he is an atua ("god") or personification of the spirit/strength of the sea. He is the son of Ranginui (the sky father) and Papatūānuku (the earth mother).

Gullible eggs (reprise)

Toetoe: a large, grassy coastal plant, genus Cortaderia, common to coastal Aotearoa and known colloquially as 'cutty-grass' due to its harsh, serrated leaves. Stands of toetoe make dry tunnels ideal for hiding, but Aotearoa's children are wary of the vicious, deep cuts it may inflict. *Guy Fawkes:* here refers to the 'celebration' of the failed Gunpowder Plot of 1605, aka Bonfire Night, marked in colonised New Zealand much as it is in the UK; on the 5th of November, with public displays of fireworks and backyard parties. Very recently, public fireworks displays have been discontinued in favour of a Matariki (Māori astral new year) public holiday. Of note for this poem: the author was born early on the 6th of November, due to a fireworks misadventure.

The coast road is closed

The continuous road along the south coast of Te Whanganui-a-Tara runs right next to Te Raukawa (Cook Strait), flanked by steep hills and ridges. Storms causing immense breakers to disrupt the road are frequent, more so in recent years. Without addressing current rates of climate change, indications are that within 10 years these roads may be untenable. The remains of gun emplacements from the 1930/40s are also found along high ridgelines on this coast.

Take two (2) in the morning, after disclosing as needed: ii

Kuramarotini: often called the 'stolen wife of Kupe'. In Māori oral history, Kupe is the original discoverer of Aotearoa, who set sail from Hawaiki on his voyage of discovery after tricking Kuramarotini into his canoe. Note that in this poem, she takes her place as a powerful woman with a voice in her own right when speaking to the author's friend, who felt her own roots as a descendant – rather than occupying her more usual secondary role as 'wife of Kupe'.

The giant fish takes back the myth

This poem refers to Te Ika-a-Māui (*the fish of Māui*): the name given to the North Island of Aotearoa in the story of Māui, the legendary figure who, in Aotearoa's creation myth, fished up this island. The shape of Te Whanganui-a-Tara is seen as her jaws. Most children learn this story, yet despite walking on her to this day, the fish herself bears no name of her own.

Franz Josef glacier 2020 (will they say)

This glacier's Māori name is Kā Roimata o Hine Hukatere (*the tears of Hine Hukatere*), after the traditional story of a woman mourning her lover lost to an avalanche. The English name is used in the title in reference to the drastic, ugly changes colonisation/overpopulation and tourism wreak on fragile landscapes like her. References in this poem centre around the glacier's state of rapid retreat since 2008 due to global warming. She is predicted to lose 38% of her mass by 2100. During the Australian bushfires of 2020, her face turned brown/orange with drifted ash and dust. 'A mountain stokes the forge' is a reference to the layer of ash from the eruption of Whakaari volcano in Dec 2019, and the author speculates that the total lockdowns which stopped mass transport during the global pandemic in 2020 may have laid down a new record of abruptly clean tears.

Matariki (southern right)

Matariki is the Māori name for the star cluster Pleiades. When this clutser rises in June/July, it marks the beginning of a new year. The name is an abbreviation of Ngā Mata o te Ariki Tāwhirimātea (*the eyes of the chief Tāwhirimātea*). In Te Whanganui-a-Tara, a tohorā (southern right whale) has repeatedly visited the harbour at this time, delaying a local public fireworks display launched from a harbour barge.

Earthquake weather

Te Whanganui-a-Tara is notoriously prone to earthquakes, lying along the border of two tectonic plates on a very active fault line. It is also the windiest capital city in the world. *Rūaumoko* is the personification of the spirit of earthquakes, volcanoes, and seasons.

Matariki (the winter-maid)

Also see note above about Matariki. *Hine-Takurua* is one of the two wives of the sun, Tamanuiterā (aka Rā). After winter solstice, the sun begins his journey away from her, back to his summer wife, Hine-Raumati, who lives in the North. *Kumarā* is akin to a sweet potato (morning glory rather than nightshade family), was an important staple crop, and is popular roasted/steamed. Common varieties are orange, red, or yellow – orange is the author's favourite.

Bringing back that which is lost

Moa: A huge flightless bird of the order *Dinornithiformes*. Once endemic to Aotearoa, species stood up to twelve feet tall. Moa have been extinct since the 14th century.

That which can be made visible

In memory of the 22 people lost in the eruption of Whakaari, 9 December 2019. The remains of two people were unable to be retrieved, and remain on the island to this day. One translation of the te reo Māori name of the volcano forms the title of this poem.

Pōhutukawa

These distinctive native trees (*Metrosideros excelsa*) are prolific throughout Aotearoa, with dense, brilliant clusters of scarlet blooms consisting mostly of stamens. They reach peak flowering at midsummer, in December/January, and are known colloquially as Aotearoa's 'Christmas Tree', popular on cards and giftwrap. They are an important tree to Māori, as the spirits who leap from the northernmost tip of Aotearoa (see also 'Travelling light') do so from their branches. Rarely, a yellow or white variety is seen. When the stamens of the more usual red trees drop en masse after flowering, they form beautiful drifts and rivers of scarlet on the ground. Huge examples thrive around the coasts where the author loves to tread the red at summer's end.

About the author

Ankh Spice is a sea-obsessed poet from Aotearoa New Zealand. More than a hundred of his poems have been published internationally, and his work has been nominated eight times for the Pushcart Prize and/or Best of the Net. He was a joint winner of The Poetry Archive's WorldView competition in 2020.

His work explores a range of themes close to his heart: environmental change, mental health, trauma, conscience, identity, queerness, physicality, mythology, natural science, spirituality, directed attention, language as magic, the unique landscape of Aotearoa, the persistent briefness of being human, and his second enduring love, the ocean.

Ankh has a micro-booklet of poems forthcoming with Hedgehog Press as part of their Stickleback series in late 2021, and a two-part chapbook of short imagistic poems paired with his own nature photography in progress with an independent UK press – further details to be announced in 2022.

If he's not out on the coast of Te Whanganui-a-Tara, you'll find him and his poems at www.ankhspice-seagoatscreamspoetry.com.

The Water Engine is Ankh's debut poetry collection.